I0079636

THE HESSE-CASSEL

MIRABACH REGIMENT

IN THE

AMERICAN REVOLUTION

Bruce E. Burgoyne

HERITAGE BOOKS
2008

HERITAGE BOOKS

AN IMPRINT OF HERITAGE BOOKS, INC.

Books, CDs, and more—Worldwide

For our listing of thousands of titles see our website
at
www.HeritageBooks.com

Published 2008 by
HERITAGE BOOKS, INC.
Publishing Division
100 Railroad Ave. #104
Westminster, Maryland 21157

Copyright © 1998 Bruce E. Burgoyne

All rights reserved. No part of this book may be reproduced or
transmitted in any form or by any means, electronic or mechanical,
including photocopying, recording or by any information storage
and retrieval system without written permission from the author,
except for the inclusion of brief quotations in a review.

International Standard Book Numbers
Paperbound: 978-0-7884-0940-0
Clothbound: 978-0-7884-7108-7

Table of Contents

Preface

The Mirbach Infantry Regiment was one of the Hessian units sold into English service by Friedrich II of Hesse-Cassel in 1776 when England needed troops to suppress the rebellion in the American colonies. For all units from Hesse-Cassel, the regimental quartermaster maintained the regimental journal, or as termed in today's American forces, the unit history. The regimental quartermaster of the Mirbach Regiment was August Schmidt.

The Mirbach Regiment was not engaged in battle as frequently as some other units, but suffered combat losses far in excess of most others, as the result of an unsuccessful, primarily Hessian, attack on Fort Mercer, also known as Fort Red Bank, in New Jersey.

Fortunately the journal of a junior officer, Ensign, later Lieutenant, Karl Friedrich Rueffer, of Melsungen in Hesse-Cassel, is still available. Rueffer served in the Mirbach Regiment throughout the war and participated in all major activities involving the regiment. Thus his journal confirms, or is confirmed by the regimental journal. Unfortunately, Rueffer's journal ends with the Mirbach Regiment entering winter quarters in New York in December 1777. As an appendix to his journal, Rueffer lists all Hesse-Cassel officer deaths which occurred during 1776 and 1777.

Editorial Procedures

In making these translations, I have changed dates to a consistent form, added an e to vowels a, o, and u to indicate umlauts, and used parentheses in the text when so used by the authors. My comments are in brackets. The spelling of names have been left in most cases as recorded by the authors, which indicates that the spelling was often dependent on the author's preference. Perhaps it should be noted here that Hesse-Cassel had compulsory education in 1725. By using brackets I have eliminated the need for disruptive footnotes. I have not provided a bibliography as most libraries and computers make such information easily available.

Acknowledgments

Inge Auerbach and Otto Froehlich, as always, must be thanked for the extensive work done in providing identification of personnel in the Hesse-Cassel units. Bob Cowan of Lake Kiowa, Texas has given me much good guidance and has also helped to identify many of the English and American officers. And John F. DeBardeleben provided new information on his ancestors of the von Bardeleben family. The personnel at Heritage Books, Inc., in Bowie, Maryland, have once again enabled me to make my translations available to those who do not have the time, training, or inclination to translate the German documents, and their editorial assistance has made for a better, more readable final product, And, finally, but most important of all, the support and assistance of my wife Marie, allows me to continue making these translations which I feel are important to an understanding of the American struggle for independence.

Bruce E. Burgoyne
Dover, DE

Introduction

The translations which follow provide the names of regimental officers, the populated places along the march route to and from the German port, ship assignments when the Mirbach Regiment went to sea, and accounts of regimental involvement in the Battles of Long Island and Fort Washington, as well as General William Howe's 1777 Philadelphia Campaign and the catastrophic attack on Red Bank

As always, I recommend that for serious researchers, the original material be checked to verify my translations.

There seems to be no necessity of repeating the contents of the journals here, and I can provide no additional information about the authors.

Journal
of the
Illustrious Young von Lossberg Regiment

prior to 1780 the von Mirbach Regiment
Beginning on
1 March 1776
and ending on
30 May 1784

Maintained by
August Schmidt
Regimental Quartermaster
of the Noted Regiment

Note: As always, I recommend that serious researchers verify my translation by returning to the source document. Due to the many very dark pages from which I worked and the cases where the writing on the reverse side bled through, making translation difficult, I can not guarantee the accuracy of the entire translation.

Journal of the Young von Lossberg Regiment
Initially the von Mirbach Regiment

- - - - - - -

Beginning in 1776 - As it pleased Our Most Gracious Lord, His Serene Highness, most graciously to order an auxiliary troop of 12,000 men into the service of the Crown of England, in North America, and as the von Mirbach Regiment, (later to be designated the Young von Lossberg Regiment), with other regiments was assigned thereto, it received the necessary recruits to bring the companies to full strength, and was supplied with the necessary field equipment, so that it would be ready to march by mid-February. As a result, this occurred at Melsungen, which was then the regimental quarters area.

1 March - On this day the regiment moved to Waldau and Crumbach.

2 March - A day of rest.

3 March - The regiment marched to Landwehrhagen in Electoral Hannover.

4 March - From the above place to Patterode and Guentersen.

5 March - To Moringen, Tudinghausen, Oberndorf, Nienhagen, and Luetterbeck.

6 March - A day of rest.

7 March - To Alfeld, a small city in Bishopric Hildesheim.

8 March - To Schulenberg, Jeinsen, and Roessing.

9 March - Through Hannover, where the Leine River was crossed, and from there to Herrnhausen, to Ricklingen, Meyenfeld, and Horst, Garbsen, and Freilingen.

10 March - A day of rest.

11 March - To Holtorf and Erichshagen, District of Woelpe.

12 March - To Hoya, where the Weser River was crossed.

13 March - A day of rest.

14 March - To Syke, Okel, Barrien, and Osterholz

15 March - Through Bremen where the river was recrossed. To Massell, Moehr, Grambke, and Oslepshausen.

16 March - To Osterholz, Lilien[thal], Buschhausen, and Scharmbeck.

17 March - - A day of rest.

18 March - To Kuhstedt, Osterweder, and Giele.

Journal of the Mirbach Regiment

19 March - To Otell Lippstadt and Barchel, in which latter place a thriving animal breeding was encountered.

20 March - The regiment entered cantonments in Bederkesa, where it remained until 25 March.

26 March - The march proceeded from Bederkesa to Welsdorf, Schiffdorf, and Bramel.

27 March - The regiment received orders to march to Bremerlehe to be mustered.

28 March - The regiment was mustered there and was administered the oath [to the English Crown] by the English representative Colonel [William] Faucitt. Then the regiment returned to the last three mentioned places and remained in cantonments until 6 April.

6 April - The regiment marched, on orders, to Lehe, Spaden, Debstedt, and Laven and remained there until 16 April.

16 April - The eleven previously mustered regiments, including the three grenadier battalions, minus one company of the Knyphausen Fusilier Regiment, under the command of His Excellence, Lieutenant General von Heister, having embarked on 42 ships, sailed from Lehe to Portsmouth.

19 April - The regiment was embarked on the following ships.

On *Albion* - Major General [Werner] von Mirbach, Captain [Wilhelm Erdmann] von Bogatzky, Lieutenants [Friedrich Andreas] Schotten, [adjutant] and [Ludwig Wilhelm August von] Boyneburg, and Regimental Surgeon [Karl Konrad] Gechter.

On *Greyhound* - Colonel [Johann August] von Loos, Major [Hans Moritz] von Biesenrodt, Captain [Johann Kaspar] Riess, 2nd Lieutenants [Karl Henrich] von Toll and [Johann Konrad] Schraidt, and Ensign [Hans Friedrich] von Biesenrodt.

On *Henry* - Lieutenant Colonel [Ernst Rudolph] von Schieck, Captain [David] Reichhold, 2nd Lieutenant [Karl Friedrich] von Wurmb, and Ensigns [Karl Friedrich] Rueffer and [Johann Georg] Wiessenmueller.

On *Union* - Captain [Johann Wilhelm] Endemann, Captain Krug, Artillery Lieutenant [Friedrich August] Broescke, Ensign [Erhard] von Drach, Auditor [Johannes] Heinemann, and me, the Regimental Quartermaster [Schmidt].

Journal of the Mirbach Regiment

On *Eagle* - Lieutenant [Johann Konrad] Riemann, Ensign [Karl Wilhelm] von Bulzingsloewen, also Lieutenants [Andreas] Wiederhold and [Johann Friedrich Wilhelm] Briede, Ensign [Wilhelm] von Drach, and Auditor [Friedrich] Mueller of the von Knyphausen Fusilier Regiment, and War Councilor Lorenz and several of the commissariat.

From 19 April to 12 May - The regiment lay at anchor in the harbor at Lehe. During the night of 25 to 26 April a very severe storm struck, so that most of the ships of our fleet broke loose from their anchors. The ship *Henry*, which at three o'clock in the afternoon of 26 April lost three anchors, was driven ashore at twelve o'clock at night in the region of Geestendorf, and due to the force of the waves, was stuck fast, so that despite all the sailors' efforts, it could not be refloated. Therefore it was made lighter by removing all the people and the baggage to other ships on 30 April. On 2 May the ship was refloated and on 6 May the men were returned on board and on 9 May no one could go ashore as the departure was at hand.

13 May - The signal was given to raise the anchor and to set sail. We sailed for about an hour from our first place, but then because of contrary winds, we had to anchor again near Dettenst, a Danish village, and had to remain there until 17 May.

18 May - At three o'clock in the morning we received the first signal by a cannon shot, and at five o'clock the second signal, to sail, and did so. The wind was northeast and so favorable that we sailed eight to ten miles per hour. At eight o'clock we had not only passed the dangerous sandbanks in the water, but in this time had reached the North Sea. At ten o'clock we lost sight of land and most of the troops had developed the usual seasickness.

19 May - Nothing of consequence occurred and we continued to sail with a favorable wind.

20 May - At three o'clock in the afternoon we saw the coast of England, actually the County of Kent, which lay to our right, and shortly thereafter, Dover Castle, sitting on a high hill. The city of this name, however, remained out of sight, (because a thick fog arose). Later we saw the coast of France , but also, because of thick air, we could not see Calais. At eight o'clock in the evening we entered the [English] Channel, and as it was already dark, nothing more could be seen, except the fire of the lighthouse at Dungeness, to our right, which insured the safety of the ships.

21 May - Toward nine o'clock we saw the coast of the Isle of Wight, and at one o'clock we entered Portsmouth harbor. We had seen the city a few hours earlier. We were to have joined the first fleet there, but after taking on water and other provisions, the fleet of 150 transport ships, escorted by eight warships, had sailed to America already on 6 May.

22 May - During the morning three English commissioners from the navy, who were ordered by Admiral Douglas, inspected the damage which had occurred to the ship *Henry* on 26 April. They found the ship unsatisfactory as a transport to America. Therefore the men were transferred in the afternoon. Lieutenant von Schieck, Lieutenant von Wurmb, Ensign Rueffer, and 125 men were transferred to the ship *Molly*.

Captain Reichhold and Ensign Wiessenmueller and 45 men were transferred to the *Rockingham*, and forty-five men to the *Charming Nancy*. As there were no officers on the last mentioned ship, Captain Krug of the Artillery, Lieutenants Wiederhold and Briede, and Ensign von Drach, as well as the company of the von Knyphausen Regiment which had been held back, and Ensign von Drach of the von Mirbach Regiment were embarked from the ships *Union* and *Eagle*.

Here we received fresh beef for two days, which greatly pleased our soldiers, as they had salted provisions for the previous four weeks.

Note - Aboard ship, in addition to the four pounds of zwieback and bottle of rum daily, for every six men, there was issued

On Sunday - eight pounds of pork and two ladles of peas

On Monday - two pounds of barley and two pounds of zwieback, or in place of the latter, one-half pound of butter and four-fifths of a pound of Dutch cheese, or one pound of butter, or instead of butter, cheese

Tuesday - two pounds of beef or six pounds of flour, one pound of rice, and one-half pound of salt

Wednesday - two ladles of peas, two pounds of barley, one-half pound of zwieback, and two-thirds of a pound of cheese, or as above

Thursday - like on Sunday

Friday - like on Wednesday

Saturday - like on Tuesday.

In addition, daily during the first days, as much small beer as an individual wished, but this lasted only about six days, until we were issued rum and water, and if the voyage takes too long, we will drink water.

23 May - We remained here, lying in the harbor and only on the following day,

24 May - was the anchor raised and the entire fleet, consisting of 27 sail, assembled at St. Helens, where the anchor was dropped again.

25 May - At four o'clock in the morning the escort frigate *Repulse*, of 36 cannons, which had previously belonged to France and been captured by the English, gave the signal to get underway. One hour later we set sail, but because the wind died completely, we had to anchor at Sundown Bay. About four o'clock in the afternoon the anchor was raised again, but because a strong west wind arose, which was contrary to our continuing, we turned back to St. Helens.

26 May - We sailed at daybreak, again to the region of Sundown Bay, where we had anchored the previous day. At about five o'clock in the afternoon we raised the previously lowered anchor and set sail.

27 May - We thought at daybreak that we would have lost sight of the Isle of Wight, but became aware that during the night we had traveled few miles, as we could still see that island. The exceptional calm was the cause that the ship had hardly moved and was the cause of the admiral finding it necessary, at four o'clock in the afternoon, to anchor, which was done. In about two hours, however, the anchor was raised again and we sailed from the coast of England with a southeast wind.

28 May - We lost sight of land. The captain of a ship coming from America, which our fleet encountered, told us that he had seen the first fleet, consisting of 200 ships, about fourteen days previously. It had been joined by 42 ships from Scotland, and had been in the best condition when he lost sight of it.

29 May - A very strong west wind arose, for which reason, in order that we should not fear being driven on land and stranded, on this and the following day we tacked and seemed to be driven backward. During the night of 29 to 30 May, six ships, which had not noticed the signal lights displayed by the ship leading the fleet, became separated from us. The west wind which persisted for several days had driven us back so that on

Journal of the Mirbach Regiment

31 May - prior to sunset, to our not unexpected surprise, we saw the coast of England once again. Two of the ships, which had become separated from the fleet, rejoined today, and one, which was loaded with provisions and which had lost the mainmast due to the strong wind, had fortunately reentered the harbor at Falmouth with everyone on board, according to reports received.

1 June - There was a complete calm during the morning, but a strong wind arose from the northwest during the afternoon. The three ships still missing, including the *Albion*, on which were to be found General von Mirbach and the English agent, rejoined the fleet today.

2 June - The same calm as yesterday set in again. Toward evening the northwest wind arose also.

3 June - The entire fleet sailed out of the channel with a strong west wind.

From 4 to 25 June - Nothing of note occurred. We had generally west winds, which made our journey very slow and difficult, as we always had to tack.

26 June - Some ships of the fleet saw the Azores Islands, which lay to our right and Madeira to our left.

From 27 June to 20 July - Nothing of consequence occurred. For more than ten days the ocean was calm, which the English seamen said was unusual.

21 July - A fishing sloop from Newfoundland, which came to our fleet, brought news, however, it remained a secret to us.

From 22 to and including 24 July - Nothing special occurred.

25 July - The frigate chased after a ship, but could not overtake it. However, as soon as the frigate returned to us, the commanders were ordered, as of today, to maintain a watch on deck consisting of one officer, two non-commissioned officers, one drummer, and twenty privates, with loaded weapons, both day and night, which was done. As we were half way on our voyage this struck us as very strange, however the precaution was necessary as the commodore was aware of enemy privateers in the near vicinity.

Between 25 July and 5 August - Nothing new occurred. We sailed with changing wind and weather.

5 August - At daybreak we saw a large ship. The frigate sailed toward the same and brought it back. It was an English frigate of 20 cannons, which had been sent out recently, and which soon left us.

Journal of the Mirbach Regiment

6, 7, and 8 August - Nothing special occurred which would be worth noting.

9 August - We became aware that the sea began to change color and became green like the North Sea. The seamen assured us that it was caused by the bottom and that we were no longer far from land. The lead was cast immediately. We found bottom today at only thirty fathoms.

10 August - The weather was fine and the wind favorable.

11 August - Three strange ships sailed directly at us. At first we thought they were privateers, but as they came closer, we soon noticed that they were English frigates that were to escort us to the coast. All day long we saw a lot of grass in the ocean, which was another sign that the shore was not very distant.

12 August - At two o'clock in the morning the commodore notified the fleet by firing twelve cannon shots that we were close to land and to hold the sails against the wind and not to sail farther during the night, and to be aware of the danger. At daybreak we saw the lighthouse at Sandy Hook. To the left and right lay a strong fleet, which according to later reports had sailed from Portsmouth on 6 May. As we then drew closer to it, the large warships lying there were saluted by our frigates with thirteen cannon shots, which greeting was immediately answered with eleven of the same. Then both fleets turned and sailed to Staten Island, where we encountered a fleet of 300 ships at anchor. The English army was camped on this island and the fleet lay at anchor between Staten and Long Island, just in sight of New York, about two and one-half miles from the city. It was a marvelous sight to see such a fleet of more than 300 ships lying together.

13 August - The entire corps remained aboard the ships.

14 August - The Jaegers and Grenadiers debarked during the afternoon.

15 August - The remaining regiments landed, and just like the Grenadiers, entered camp on Staten Island, opposite the Englanders.

16 August - Everything was quiet.

17 August - First the regiments received land provisions; on the express order of the commanding general, two days' issue of fresh beef was the first item delivered.

Journal of the Mirbach Regiment

18 August - Today there was a heavy cannonade, which the three warships, which sailed to New York, had to withstand from the fort, but which did little damage. The warships, during this event, captured an enemy ship lying in the North River.

19, 20, and 21 August - The regiment remained in camp on Staten Island.

22 August - Fifteen thousand men of those regiments camped on Staten Island, among whom were the Hessian Grenadiers and Jaegers, were carried across to Long Island in small boats.

23 August - An attack occurred on the mentioned island, which resulted in American losses of about 100 men.

24 August - The regiment received an order to be prepared to march.

25 August - The brigades of Generals Stirn and von Mirbach, to which the regiment was also assigned, were also transferred to Staten Island [Long Island ?] in boats.

26 August - The regiment changed camp and moved far inland. Firing from the outposts throughout the day.

27 April - An attack occurred at daybreak against the Americans posted in a large and very thick woods not far from the village of Flatbush. They also lost five cannons and one howitzer, six flags, and a large number of small weapons. In this affair, the Hessians captured two generals, [John] Sullivan and [William Alexander, Lord] Stirling, (of which the latter was taken to General [Leopold] von Heister's quarters at Flatbush by a non-commissioned officer and two privates of the regiment), among many other officers, non-commissioned officers, and more than 800 privates. The regiment remained lying in bivouac before the mentioned woods, and on

28 August - at daybreak the searching through the woods was resumed in order to find the rebels who were still therein and without help. At one o'clock the regiment returned to its camp. At four-thirty in the afternoon on this day we changed our camp and moved forward about two and one-half miles. A battery was located here, opposite the enemy defenses, provided with heavy cannons which were to cannonade the enemy as soon as they were ready.

29 August - We remained in place, completely idle. The outposts were constantly engaged, however.

9

Journal of the Mirbach Regiment

30 August - During the night the enemy evacuated all their works and returned to New York.

31 August - We entered Brooklyn upon the report that all the enemy defenses had been evacuated.

From 1 to and including 12 September - Nothing of note occurred. Five warships sailed between New York and Long Island during full daylight on 12 September. A heavy cannonade then developed from both sides.

13 September - The commander-in-chief, Sir William Howe, announced in orders how the enemy will soon be attacked and furthermore that the troops should demonstrate the same ardor and bravery displayed in the battle on 27 August.

14 September - We received the order to be prepared to march out at once and to be provided with rations for two days.

15 September - We marched out of camp at three o'clock in the morning. The tents remained standing and all baggage was left behind. Toward eight o'clock we halted, and at nine o'clock saw on a narrow inlet, called Newtown Creek, which runs from the East River far into Long Island, a number of boats on which were gradually embarked all the army's grenadiers and light infantry, as well as the English Guards. At eleven o'clock they began moving and about twelve o'clock noon they moved up the East River. Three [or possibly five] warships simultaneously directed such a heavy fire against the enemy shore, that the rebels had to vacate the area and withdraw far inland.

16 September - We were also transferred onto York Island in boats and followed the enemy on foot. During the evening we learned that the enemy had left New York, spiked all the cannons in his key defenses, and some days before, had taken all the bells from the churches.

17 September - The Stein Brigade, consisting of the Hereditary Prince, von Donop, and von Mirbach Regiments, entered camp at Bloomingdale just behind the Hessian Grenadiers and formed the second defensive line.

From yesterday until 22 September we remained peacefully in camp.

22 September - A corps of 12,000 men, including the regiment, marched to the North River in order to attack an enemy position called Paulus Hook, on the bank in New Jersey, opposite the city of New

Journal of the Mirbach Regiment

York. However, because the warships necessary for the attack could not approach near enough due to contrary wind, we returned to our respective camps during the evening.

23 September - Paulus Hook was actually attacked and captured by the English regiments. On the other hand, our regiment and the other two, Hereditary Prince and von Donop, remained in camp on the occupied terrain until 30 September.

30 September - The camp of the Stirn Brigade was changed and we set up our tents ahead of the Grenadiers, close behind the outposts.

From 1 to 27 October - Everything was peaceful. On 2 October three warships sailed up the North River and dropped anchor near the ships already lying there, and in the region of our camp. After a few days, actually on 6 October, they went farther up the river, during which passage, from both enemy occupied banks a heavy cannonade was directed against them. According to the information that was spread, whenever possible they were to provide a diversion for the advance from Canada of General [John] Burgoyne.

During the night from 10 to 11 October, General [William] Howe and the largest part of the army went toward Connecticut in 200 boats.

27 October - We made an attack against Fort Washington and remained there overnight.

28 October - We remained under arms close to the enemy defenses until evening and then pulled back into our camp.

29 October - Nothing happened.

30 October - The English General [James] Grant was detached to Connecticut with his brigade. Therefore the Stirn Brigade had to change camp and then until 15 November, we remained undisturbed.

15 November - Toward evening we received the order to be under arms at five o'clock tomorrow morning.

16 November - At daybreak, in accordance with the order received, we were under arms. We did not begin our march until the arrival of [Hugh,] Lord Percy's adjutant at General Stirn's. He reported to us that we would attack the enemy's defenses today, which occurred with a heavy loss. The regiment was to capture the Rock Redoubt. However, the enemy vacated that position upon our approach, and withdrew to a defense of three lines, one behind the other, and Fort Washington. On the other hand, the loss by Lieutenant General [Wilhelm] von Knyphausen's Corps, which attacked the enemy

11

at the same time from the side toward Kingsbridge, was considerable. Under that attack, the enemy vacated all his defenses on that side, and pulled back into Fort Washington, which held out only a few hours before capitulating. The defenders, consisting of 2,371 men, had to lay down their weapons before the Koehler Grenadier Battalion, which afterward occupied the fort. In such a glorious manner, this day ended. During the night the Mirbach Regiment had to escort the prisoners to Harlem, where they spent two days being guarded in barns. From there they were taken to New York under escort of an English regiment. Thereafter we entered our camp, remaining there until 3 December, when we entered winter quarters.

3 December - The Stirn Brigade marched to New York and entered winter quarters. The regiment was assigned in the houses on King's Street, which for our troops were better living quarters than the barracks.

From 6 December 1776 to 22 May in the following year of 1777 - The regiment remained lying in winter quarters, and nothing of importance occurred.

23 May - The New York garrison received orders to be prepared to embark at a moment's notice.

24 May to 3 June - The regiment held itself ready to march at once.

3 June - It was announced in orders that the Leib Regiment, recently arrived from Rhode Island, the von Donop Regiment, and the von Mirbach Regiment, and six English regiments were to be prepared to embark at once.

4 June - The English regiments began embarking, and on

5 June - the regiment embarked on the following ships:

On *Jenny*: Colonel Block, Captain Rothe, Lieutenants von Toll and Schraidt, Ensign von Drach, and Regimental Surgeon Gechter

On *New Blessing*: Lieutenant Colonel von Schieck, Captains Reichhold and Krug, Lieutenant von Boyneburg, and Ensign Wiessenmueller

On *Mermaid*: Major Biesenrodt, Captain von Bogatzky, Lieutenant Rueffer, Ensigns Biesenrodt and Berner, and also none other than myself, the regimental quartermaster.

On *Lord Howe*: Captain Endemann, Lieutenants Riemann and von Wurmb, Ensign Bulzingsloewen, and Chaplain Virnau.

Journal of the Mirbach Regiment

6 June - We remained lying at anchor in New York harbor.

7 June - We set sail from Sandy Hook at ten o'clock in the morning, and then sailed around Staten Island to Amboy in New Jersey, where we had to anchor at evening.

8 June - We debarked at Amboy and entered camp there, where we remained until 12 June.

12 June - We marched away from that place and entered camp near Brunswick, constructed two redoubts on the Raritan River, and after receiving orders, on the following day

14 June - at two o'clock in the morning, we began our march to Middlebush. We remained here until 19 June, under the open sky, because all our baggage, including the tents, had been left behind in Brunswick. Colonel Block, who until now commanded the regiment, due to poor health, had to give up his command at this place and Lieutenant Colonel von Schieck took over.

19 June - At daybreak we marched back and again settled on this side of the Raritan River. The rear guard was occasionally disturbed during our return, but suffered no casualties.

20 to 21 June - We remained here in camp.

22 June - On the same day the entire army moved back to Amboy from Brunswick. The Stirn Brigade and six English regiments were transferred across to Staten Island and entered camp at Prince's Bay, where we stayed until 24 June.

24 June - At eight o'clock in the morning the Stirn Brigade received orders to board the previously assigned ships once again, which was done immediately.

25 June - At about three o'clock in the afternoon the ship's captain received orders to sail. At the same time Captain [Friedrich von] Muenchhausen brought an order that we were to be prepared to debark at any moment. Nevertheless, we sailed to Amboy and the troops were landed at twelve o'clock at night. *New Blessing*, on board which was Lieutenant Colonel von Schieck, the regimental commander, ran aground and was refloated during the flood tide with the help of some flatboats. As soon as the brigade had assembled at Amboy, we marched away on

26 June - in columns from the right. Our march was to Woodbridge and Westfield, both of which places are eighteen English miles from Amboy. According to confirmed reports the enemy lost

Journal of the Mirbach Regiment

600 men and three metal cannons, two of which were captured by the Minnigerode Grenadier Battalion and the third by the English Guards. During this expedition, two non-commissioned officers and two privates of our regiment, who were escorting provisions, and who were straggling, were captured.

27 June - At eleven o'clock in the morning we moved back with the remaining troops to Rahway, six miles from Amboy, where we spent the night in bivouac. The heat was so great that one man from the regiment died on the march.

28 June - We continued the return march to Amboy and embarked in the previously assigned ships lying in Prince's Bay. This entire expedition occurred, in looking back, as a result of trying to draw the enemy into battle. However, he did not consider this advisable and remained quietly in the so-called Blue Mountains, behind his well-constructed defenses.

29 and 30 June - We remained lying at anchor.

1 July - We again raised the anchor, but because of contrary winds, we again had to anchor. Toward three o'clock the anchor was raised and we arrived at King's Ferry on Staten Island at seven o'clock in the evening. However, we had to remain on board the ship until 20 July. On the eleventh Lieutenant Schotten, who served as an adjutant to the sick Major General von Mirbach, who had remained in New York, came to the regiment as he wished to take part in the expedition, and remained on board the ship *Mermaid*, and circulated the order on 13 July to the regiments, battalions, and corps, that beginning tomorrow, 14 July, no one should leave the ships, which was complied with until

20 July - at ten o'clock in the morning, when the signal was given to raise the anchor. We had hardly sailed for one hour until we again had to anchor due to contrary wind. The army, to insure success, consisted of 44 battalions.

21 July - We again raised the anchor and sailed to Sandy Hook, and the entire fleet, excluding the warships, gathered and anchored near Long Island.

22 July - We remained lying at anchor in this area.

23 July - At six o'clock in the morning Admiral [Richard, Lord] Howe, with a favorable north wind, joined us with all the warships assigned to the fleet, which had not previously assembled, and the entire fleet, which consisted of 257 ships, sailed into the ocean after having raised the anchor on the previously given signal. We at once turned right, toward the south, which made us think our course was toward Philadelphia.

24 to 30 July - Nothing of consequence occurred.

30 July - We saw the coast of Maryland and at twelve o'clock noon today we entered Delaware Bay. We sailed as far as Cape Henlopen, where the lighthouse for Philadelphia stands, which was on our left. We began to tack and did so until dark, without sailing farther into the bay. Before it became completely dark, the admiral gave a signal, whereupon we turned back toward the sea. On the following morning,

31 July - we still saw the lighthouse and the coast of Maryland, both of which we soon lost from sight and we appeared to be in the open sea again. During our approach the Americans, from the mentioned lighthouse, watched through their telescopes. A signal was given and we then turned toward the south as before, and sailed with a constantly contrary wind until

14 August - when finally, at noon, we saw Cape Charles. About eleven o'clock in the evening we anchored in the vicinity of this cape.

15 August - We also saw Cape Henry.

16 August - The anchor was raised again and we sailed into Chesapeake Bay at about three o'clock in the afternoon. The Maryland shore was to our right and that of Virginia to our left. We continued to sail into the bay, but for fear of taking a wrong passage, anchored during the night.

From 17 to 21 August - Nothing of note occurred.

21 August - At nine o'clock in the morning to the left, in the Virginia region, we saw the pretty little city called Arundel, or Annapolis, which has a harbor. The rebels had thrown up defensive positions and raised two American flags therein.

22 August - We arrived near Elk's Ferry, where we remained lying at anchor on this and the following day.

24 August - The light troops began to debark at Elk's Ferry.

25 August - At five o'clock in the afternoon a small part of our regiment was landed. However, the rest had to remain aboard ship all night due to a strong storm, as Admiral Howe would not risk more. All the previously landed troops had to spend the night without tents.

26 August - The rest of the troops, who had not landed on the previous day were put ashore, and on the same day we received all of our baggage. Because of a scarcity of level ground, the camp was set up in an irregular manner.

27 August - We changed our camp and formed it in a regular manner. The advance guard moved forward. Lieutenant General von Knyphausen covered the Elk River, where all the transport ships were, which had previously carried the troops.

From 28 to 30 August - We remained peacefully in our camp.

31 August - We were carried across Elk River in flatboats to Cecil Courthouse, and marched the same day to Cecil Church, where we set up camp.

1 September - We remained there in camp.

2 September - At five o'clock in the morning we marched six miles farther to Bohema in Pennsylvania.

3 September - We went to Aiken's Tavern, where we joined the main army, after the Jaegers had a brief skirmish with the Americans.

4 September - About four o'clock in the afternoon we received the order that all non-essential baggage and tents were to be taken to the ships, which was done in the greatest haste. The officers of each company were allowed eleven musketeer tents. The non-commissioned officers and privates, from this time on, had to lie under the open sky.

5, 6, and 7 September - We remained in the region of Aiken's Tavern.

8 September - At six o'clock in the morning the army marched from the left in three columns. At two o'clock in the afternoon we passed a pleasant, but uninhabited, little city of sixty houses called Newark. At eleven o'clock in the evening we arrived at New Garden.

9 September - At two o'clock in the afternoon the Knyphausen Division marched out from the right; the remainder of the army with General Howe, from the left, however. About twelve o'clock at night we arrived at Kennet Square, where General von Knyphausen had been ordered to halt.

10 September - At twelve o'clock noon we moved forward about two and one-half miles and set up camp.

11 September - During the night General von Knyphausen's Division marched directly toward Brandywine Hill. The main army however, had to make a great circuitous route. The entire rebel army was assembled here. Firing from their side began very early. The Queen's Rangers, which lost many men, were the advance guard. They climbed, with much difficulty and heavy losses, one height after the other, and so as not to advance too far, had to halt, just as we did. The firing was continuously sustained. Now we waited impatiently for the arrival of General Howe, who toward four o'clock directed a heavy cannon fire on the left wing, whereupon our corps moved out and near Brauntown, of Shazes Ferry, which is called Brandywine Creek, advanced with a steady haste through the water and up Brandywine Hill.

The enemy retreated in confusion and haste, and on this day we achieved a complete victory because the onset of night brought an end to the action. With this opportunity we captured eleven metal cannons and two howitzers, including two of the Hessian cannons lost at Trenton.

The enemy losses, as well as our own, remain unknown. The Stirn Brigade had two dead and three wounded, of which one of the latter was from the Mirbach Regiment.

From 12 to 16 September - We remained in bivouac at Brandywine Hill.

16 September - At three o'clock in the morning the army marched from the right. To our greatest regret, the Mirbach Regiment was separated from the main army, and hurriedly sent to the aid of Colonel von Loos, who was too weak to go against the Americans at Wilmington. At one o'clock we repassed Brandywine Hill, wading Brandywine Creek, and in the heaviest rainy weather, entered the camp near Wilmington, with the 71st Regiment of Mountain Scots, the Combined Battalion of Colonel von Loos, the hospital, and the prisoners of war.

17 September - The regiment changed camps and moved from the road to Christiana Bridge onto the hill on the right side of the road to Philadelphia, where, due to a scarcity of tents, we made huts of branches and hay. We remained here until 15 October. On 12 October all the sick and wounded and prisoners were embarked and carried to Philadelphia on the Brandywine Creek, and on the fourteenth we received orders to be ready to embark.

15 October - At six o'clock in the morning the loading of horses and baggage began, which continued until during the night. The same evening the regiment began marching also. The pickets and detachments made up the rear guard, which latter had guarded the bridge near Brandywine and also rejoined us at one o'clock during the night.

16 October - At seven-thirty in the morning we entered the available flatboats, which carried us to the ships lying at anchor. The regiment received four: *Hundred, Bristol, Mermaid,* and *Lord Howe.* On the first were: Lieutenant Colonel von Schieck, Lieutenants Schotten, Riemann, and von Toll, and Ensign von Bulzingsloewen.

On the second were: Major von Wilmowsky, Captain von Bogatzky, Lieutenants von Boyneburg and Rueffer, and Ensign Berner.

On the third were: Captain Endemann, Lieutenant von Wurmb, Ensign Wiessenmueller, Regimental Surgeon Gechter, and Chaplain Virnau.

On the fourth were: Captains Reichhold and Rothe, Ensign von Drach, and the regimental quartermaster.

At ten o'clock in the morning the anchor was raised. The wind was completely contrary, but we departed for Chester with the flood tide which was helpful. However, when the ebb set in, we had to anchor again today without reaching the mentioned little city.

17 October - At eight o'clock in the morning we raised the anchor and sought, because of the contrary wind, to get to Chester by tacking. We arrived there at two o'clock in the afternoon. The ship's captain received orders to deliver two days' provisions to the regiment.

18 October - We landed at daybreak and marched at two o'clock towards Kingstown, near the Schuylkill River, where we camped.

19 October - The enemy attacked our outposts at one o'clock in the morning but we suffered no losses.

20 October - At eleven o'clock in the morning our pickets were attacked; one man was lightly wounded. At three o'clock in the afternoon the regiment received orders to enter Philadelphia tomorrow morning at daybreak.

21 October - The regiment marched, according to orders, crossed the Schuylkill River at two o'clock in the morning, and in Philadelphia joined with three Hessian grenadier battalions - von Linsing, von

Lengercke, and von Minnigerode - and the Jaeger Corps. At daybreak the mentioned battalions and corps and our regiment, under the command of Colonel [Karl Emil Ulrich] von Donop, were transferred across the Delaware River to New Jersey. Here we learned that this command was designated to capture Fort Red Bank. As soon as we had all been transferred across, we marched off and arrived during the evening at Haddonfield, a pleasant little city nine miles from Philadelphia, where we lay in bivouac all night.

22 October - We moved out at four o'clock in the morning and took the road leading directly to the mentioned fort, which we shall certainly never forget. We arrived in the vicinity of the fort at ten o'clock, and as soon as Colonel von Donop had made the necessary preparations, at three-thirty in the afternoon he sent the English Major [Charles] Stuart and Captain [Johann Emanuel] Wagner to call upon the fort to surrender. Upon receipt of the refusal, he attacked the fort with the Lengercke Grenadier Battalion on the left, the Minnigerode Grenadier Battalion on the right, and the Mirbach Regiment in the center, and a heavy continuous cannonade. We had barely reached the outer defenses when thirteen row galleys in the Delaware River opened fire. The fire from the fort and the deep moat forced us to withdraw. As soon as we had assembled and withdrawn our cannons, while the Lengercke Grenadier Battalion provided cover, the same night we marched back across Timber Creek, without being harassed by the enemy. Toward twelve o'clock midnight, we halted in order to bandage the severely wounded, most of whom had to remain lying in the road, due to a scarcity of wagons on which to carry them. During this unsuccessful attack, the regiment suffered 36 dead, 56 wounded, and 15 taken prisoner of the non-commissioned officers and privates, and four officers were killed and three wounded. Among the dead officers were Lieutenant Colonel von Schieck, Captain von Bogatzky, and Lieutenants Riemann and von Wurmb. Among the wounded were Lieutenants Schotten and Rueffer and also Ensign Berner.

23 October - We moved out again at two o'clock in the morning. While marching we met a detachment of English light infantry and several regiments, who were heavily engaged with the enemy, repassed Haddonfield, and were transferred across the Delaware to Philadelphia, after the wounded had first been transferred and placed in a safe position. We entered a barracks in Philadelphia. On the same

Journal of the Mirbach Regiment

day Colonel [Heinrich] von Borck, who had been named interim commander of the regiment by His Excellence, Lieutenant General von Knyphausen, because of Lieutenant Colonel von Schieck's death and Major von Wilmowsky's illness, came from the von Knyphausen Regiment. The same day, at two o'clock in the afternoon, the warship *Augusta*, of 64 cannons, which was attacking Mud Island, caught fire and blew up. The sloop *Merlin*, of 18 cannons, was driven aground on the Jersey shore and then set on fire by the English themselves, and destroyed. From today until 31 October we remained lying in the barracks. On 24 October the regiment received a thank you order from the commander-in-chief for the 22 October attack which had been to our disadvantage, signed W. C. H.

31 October - The regiment moved out of the barracks and into camp in the line of the army, and remained until 15 December without anything of consequence occurring. On the eleventh of the same month orders were received to load all the baggage and horses, which was done on the following day, 12 December.

15 December - We and the 71st Regiment of Mountain Scots went aboard flatboats at one o'clock; the sick and wounded however, went aboard a two-masted sloop called *Fanny*, and were transferred to Chester.

16 December - At Chester we boarded the following named ships, with which we sailed to New York:

On *Wettby* were: Colonel von Borck, Lieutenant von Toll, Ensigns Wiessenmueller and Bulzingsloewen, as well as Ensign Abel von Wissenroth, Chaplain Virnau, and the regimental quartermaster.

On *Charming Polly* were: Major von Wilmowsky, Captains Reichhold and Rothe, as well as Lieutenants Schraidt and von Boyneburg, and Ensign von Drach.

On *Badger were*: Captain Endemann, Lieutenants Schotten and Rueffer, Ensign Berner, Auditor Heinemann, and the regimental surgeon.

17 and 18 December - We remained lying at anchor near Chester

19 December - The commander of the fleet gave a signal to depart at daybreak, which took place at once. We had only traveled a few miles however, when due to contrary wind, we had to anchor near Wilmington. About four o'clock in the afternoon we raised the anchor again and sailed onward until about seven o'clock in the evening.

Journal of the Mirbach Regiment

20 December - After raising the anchor at nine o'clock, we sailed past New Castle. Here the frigate *Apollo*, of 32 cannons, joined us. From today until 25 December we found ourselves in the open sea and nothing of interest occurred during the voyage.

25 December - We arrived in the harbor at New York at nine o'clock in the morning. We had to remain aboard ship today because of problems arranging quarters.

26 December - The regiment received orders to debark and to enter the assigned quarters on the North River, which the 57th English Regiment had occupied.

27 December - At eight o'clock in the morning we debarked and entered the quarters. The regiment was scattered over an area of about six miles.

Journal of the Mirbach Regiment

From 28 December to 9 July 1778 - In the following year nothing of consequence occurred. On 6 May Colonel [Christian] von Romrodt, who had previously been the lieutenant colonel of the Landgraf Regiment, became colonel of the regiment. He came from Rhode Island and took over command from Colonel von Borck, who had been placed in temporary command.

9 July - The regiment received the order to enter camp on the following Sunday.

10 July - We entered the camp near New York, in which we remained undisturbed until 26 November.

27 November - The regiment marched to McGowans's Pass and took the designated winter quarters in Harlem and Harlem Lane, which were two miles apart and very bad.

28 November to 2 December - Nothing of importance while in these quarters.

3 December - At four o'clock in the morning the regiment received an order from Adjutant General [Francis,] Lord Rawdon during an alarm to move out ahead of the line at Kingsbridge. The regiment moved out at eight o'clock and at eleven o'clock, near Courtland's house, awaited General [Sir William] Erskine, under whose command the regiment stood. He arrived at our location at four o'clock in the afternoon. We followed him to the 17 Mile Stone, where we bivouacked this night. In addition to our regiment, Rawdon's Volunteers, Bayard's Corps, the 7th, 44th, and 63rd Regiments, plus a squadron of Pennsylvania Dragoons and a squadron of Lord Cathcart's Legion belonged to this corps.

4 December - We continued our march toward Albany. At ten o'clock we passed Colonel [Frederick] Philipse's house, which is located between the 19 and 20 Mile Stones. After we had marched some miles farther, we saw about twenty ships on the North River. At four o'clock in the afternoon we reached Terrytown, which is a scattered out little place, lying thirty miles from New York. Upon our arrival we saw General [Henry] Clinton who had his headquarters here. No one had guessed the object of this expedition. Some believed he meant to capture Fort Defiance at West Point, which was protected by 100 cannons. Others were certain he wished to make Washington's crossing over to Jersey more difficult.

Journal of the Mirbach Regiment

5 December - The ships sailed to the region of Peekskill, six miles from Terrytown, where they fired a heavy cannonade, and shortly thereafter, a heavy firing against Jersey was seen. This day was very unpleasant and from need and a scarcity of tents, the regiment had to build huts of materials at hand.

6 December - The entire corps moved out and marched back to our former quarters. From the day of entering these quarters until

30 May 1779 - everything remained quiet at the regiment.

30 May - At eleven o'clock in the morning the colonel received an order to send two companies of the regiment to Marsten's Wharf, two to the North River by Jones' house, and one company to camp at Harlem, which order was complied with at three o'clock the same afternoon.

Between 30 May and 29 July - Nothing of importance occurred.

29 July - The two companies which had been in camp on the North River had to join those at Marsten's Wharf and set up their tents there.

8 November - The regiment moved into the huts at Marsten's Wharf, which had previously been occupied by the von Lossberg Regiment, in order to spend the winter there. However, because they were no longer in good repair, the regiment had to make necessary repairs. From today until

16 April 1780 - everything remained quiet. During the night of 16 to 17 April, Major [Johann Christian] DuPuy and 250 men who were taken from the von Mirbach and von Bose Regiments, were joined by Robinson's Corps, and ordered on an expedition into Jersey. As soon as the detachment reached the region of Fort Lee, without having encountered the least resistance, the troops were allowed to rest pending the arrival of Captain [Ernst Friedrick] von Diemar with his hussars and some cavalry, which were set across the North River near Paulus Hook. Toward noon the latter arrived at the mentioned fort, and both commands continued their march to Woodbridge, where an enemy picket was posted.

To cover the left flank, Captain Reichhold and fifty men had to occupy the bridge, and the major went with the rest of the troops to Hoppertown, where several hundred rebels were stationed. These were driven into flight without our side losing a man. During this affair, a major, five officers, and 87 men were captured. After the expedition was ended, the major and his prisoners returned. As soon as the rebels were aware that several skirmishes had taken place to their disadvantage, between our troops and theirs, all the troops in the area were assembled together, and Captain Reichhold, who commanded the rear, had one of his men killed and eleven men wounded.

Between 17 April and 28 May - Nothing significant occurred.

29 May - At seven o'clock in the evening Major DuPuy, again with 230 men from the regiments von Mirbach and von Bose, and Robinson's Corps, took the detachment to Jersey in order to attack a known enemy post. However, the rebels decided it was not advisable to remain and on reports of the approach of the mentioned troops, pulled back. Therefore the following day the detachment returned to their huts, in which the regiment had to remain camped throughout the summer, due to a shortage of tents.

17 October - This last mentioned month we received the news that we would spend the winter in the mentioned huts which were to be improved, and the mill not far from Marsten's Wharf was assigned to the regiment for Baurmeister's Company. Here we remained until

12 June 1781 - On which day the regiment, according to orders, was to be ready to march. This and the following day, however, were still spent in the huts.

14 June - Next, at five o'clock in the morning the regiment moved out, marched to Fort Knyphausen, and entered the camp on the North River. Between this day and

2 July - nothing happened, except on

3 July - in the morning, the enemy, among whom were several French regiments, was discovered in the region of our lines, by Lieutenant Colonel [Adam Ernst Carl] von Prueschenck with a detachment of Jaegers, and engaged. Therefore all the reserve pickets and all the redoubts were reinforced. The Jaegers as well as the reinforcements moved out of the line after the enemy was repulsed. At four o'clock in the afternoon they reentered the line. General Washington was seen at Spuyten Duyvil this afternoon and reconnoitered our lines.

From 4 to 21 July - Everything was quiet.

22 July - About six o'clock this morning [Donatien Vimeur,] Comte Rochambeau and General [George] Washington were seen from our lines, and according to reports received, both armies amount to about 7,000 men. They moved forward in spirited order to about half a mile from Harlem Creek, driving away the Refugees from Morrisania, and it was necessary, in the greatest danger, to retreat to Holland's Ferry. The enemy (in order to prevent this crossing) tried to capture the mentioned ferry with two 6-pound cannons, and fired continuously against the ferry, but without any serious effect. Therefore, on orders of Colonel von Romrodt, from Fort Tryon, which the regiment had occupied, shots from a 12-pound cannon drove the enemy back. Redoubt Number 8 on the far side of Harlem Creek, which Captain Broescke and Lieutenant Wiessenmueller occupied, directed cannon fire at the enemy also. The enemy army held itself back during this time but everyone had to be ready to move during this period.

23 July - It was learned that Comte Rochambeau and General Washington had their headquarters across the Bronx near Chatterton Hill.

24 July - We received news of the enemy's withdrawal to Dobb's Ferry and the Bronx, twelve miles from our lines. From this time until

24 August - we remained completely peaceful.

25 August - The 57th Regiment marched to Laurel Hill and in order to prepare three defensive positions, two companies of the regiment were detached to enter camp. Between today and 15 November nothing special occurred.

15 November - The two companies moved from the North River Hill and those companies in the Moth [?] quarters moved to Laurel Hill and the regiment entered winter quarters assigned to it. For three companies barracks were built with boards and the other two companies went into the previous old huts. All the officers had to have huts built, as those previously built were uninhabitable.

Here we remained all winter without being disturbed until 15 June 1782.

15 June 1782 - The regiment moved into camp on Laurel Hill. The Leib Company had to set up their tents in Fort George.

From 16 June to 5 November 1782 - Nothing of consequence. On the last mentioned day we received the order to enter winter quarters in New York, which was done the following day.

6 November - The regiment entered two churches, which occurred after back and forth activity. Duty in the garrison was very difficult.

Between 7 November 1782 and 7 November 1783 - During our cantonment in New York nothing of importance occurred.

On 18 July 1783 the regiment lost Lieutenant Berner, who was buried on 19 July with the military honor befitting his character. On 25 July Second Lieutenant [Carl] von Ehrenstein took his release from the regiment and sailed to Nova Scotia where he planned to settle.

8 November - The regiment was assigned ships for the voyage back to England. It received three, namely: *Palliser, George,* and *Laville,* and as no one trusted these ships for a long voyage, a protest was lodged with the result that after a few days, and actually on

12 November - two others by the names of *Supply,* which was actually a supply ship, and the transport ship *Ann were* assigned, on which the regiment finally on

21 November - embarked at nine o'clock in the morning in the following manner:

On *Supply*: Colonel von Romrodt, Lieutenant Colonel von Wilmowsky, Captains Rothe, Broescke, and Schraidt, and Lieutenant Rueffer, also Ensigns Lange, Fry, and von Bodestsky, Artillery Lieutenant Keyser, and Regimental Quartermaster Schmidt, Auditor Heinemann, and Regimental Surgeon Gechter, also the 2nd Company of Colonel von Romrodt and the company of Lieutenant Colonel von Wilmowsky, the artillery, and all those assigned to the regimental staff.

On *Ann*: Lieutenant Colonel von Biesenrodt, Captains Rodemann and von Toll, Lieutenants von Biesenrodt, von Bulzingsloewen, von Drach, and Wiessenmueller, also Provisions Administrator Ebert, and the companies of Lieutenant Colonel von Biesenrodt and Major Baurmeister.

22 November - We still lay at anchor on the ship *Supply.* In the evening a naval lieutenant brought Admiral Digby's order to get underway tomorrow morning. It so happened that the lieutenant and agent was junior to the commander of the ship *Supply*, which as mentioned was a royal armed ship, and therefore could not take command. The other ships of the fleet were opposed to the order to sail.

Journal of the Mirbach Regiment

23 November - At daybreak we raised the anchor, took our pilot on board, and sailed with a weak wind across the first bar near Sandy Hook, where, because of insufficient wind, we had to anchor.

24 November - Again at daybreak we raised the anchor and set out on our voyage with little wind. At nine o'clock we passed the second bar, and then, as we no longer needed the pilot, he was dropped off at ten o'clock, and shortly thereafter we passed the lighthouse at Sandy Hook and entered the ocean. Toward evening we lost sight of the mainland, which is called Navesink. Except for the storms and high seas at this time of year, nothing of note occurred until

18 December - On this day the packet boat *Portland*, which left New York two days after we left, reported to us that the fleet left behind us, had sailed on 25 November.

19, 20, and 21 December - The captain had the lead cast and found bottom at ninety fathoms. Therefore, as we were nearing land, the lead was cast every four hours.

23 December - At about four o'clock in the morning we saw the lighthouse at Scilly. We therefore held ourselves at a distance away from the dangerous sandbanks and rocks of that place, and toward evening reached the English Channel.

24 December - We expected to see land at daybreak, but unfortunately only at about eight o'clock in the morning did we see such to our great joy. It was Portland and about ten o'clock we saw the Isle of Wight.

25 December - The wind was so favorable that we arrived at Dover at ten o'clock, and at twelve o'clock, with a very strong wind, we arrived at our destination at The Downs, near Deal. We then anchored, and saw upon our entrance some ships which belonged to General von Wurmb's Division lying at anchor.

26 December - The ship commander traveled to the commodore's ship *Dolphin*, which had escorted von Wurmb's Division, and returned with the report that the mentioned commodore did not know how many ships of his fleet had arrived.

27 December - We remained on board the ships.

28 December - Adjutant Rueffer was sent into the city to inquire about General [Friedrich Wilhelm] von Lossberg and General von Mirbach. However, he learned that only the latter had arrived and on

Journal of the Mirbach Regiment

his ship were: Colonel [Johann Wilhelm] Schreiber, Colonel [Otto Christian Wilhelm] von Linsing, Colonel [Henrich Walrab] von Keudel, Colonel [Georg Emanuel] von Lengercke, and Lieutenant Colonel [Hans Henrich] Eitel. The ship *Ann*, which belonged to the regiment, had not yet arrived.

From 29 December 1783 to 2 January 1784 - Some of the various transport ships, under the command of General von Wurmb, sailed to Chatham. However, we had to remain here because the commodore had to wait for orders from the Admiralty before sending us on.

4 January - The ship carrying Lieutenant Colonel von Biesenroth sailed past us.

5 January - This afternoon the ship's captain received the order to sail to Sheerness, but as the pilot did not come aboard ship until this evening, we had to remain here.

6 January - In the morning the anchor was raised and we departed. Toward evening we reached Market Road, where we again anchored.

7 January - We continued our voyage and arrived at one-thirty a few miles from Sheerness, where we again had to anchor because the flood tide came to an end and the wind became contrary. The adjutant was sent to Sheerness, (as the ship had only been ordered to go this far), in order to get orders as the how we were to proceed. Upon his return we learned that it was to take place on small sloops.

8 January - In the early morning at eight o'clock we arrived at this place and sailed to Sheerness. Only during the afternoon some of the mentioned sloops took on baggage, but not until evening did the sloops arrive that were meant for the soldiers.

9 January - At daybreak, from the ship *Supply*, we were embarked on four sloops and sailed with the incoming flood tide. We arrived at Chatham at one o'clock. However, we met Lieutenant Colonel von Biesenrodt here, who was in the midst of debarking. Together we proceeded to our designated winter quarters, where we remained undisturbed until 16 March.

17 March - Not only did we receive the order to be ready to embark to go to Germany, but the ships *Betsy* and *Mary* were assigned for our use. Thereafter we remained peacefully lying in the barracks until the end of the month.

Journal of the Mirbach Regiment

1 April - Again, all of our troops from the garrison went aboard ship at Chatham. The ship *Mary* was boarded by Colonel von Romrodt, Lieutenant Colonel von Wilmowsky, Captains Rodemann, Broescke, Schraidt, Lieutenant Rueffer, Ensign Lange, also myself, the regimental quartermaster, Auditor Heinemann, Colonel von Romrodt's and Lieutenant Colonel Von Wilmowsky's Companies, and Major Baurmeister's Company, and the artillery, and members of the lower staff.

On *Betsy* were: Lieutenant Colonel von Biesenrodt, Captains Rothe and von Toll, Lieutenants von Biesenrodt, von Bulzingsloewen, and von Drach, and Ensign [Carl] von Bode, Artillery Lieutenant [Johann Georg] Kayser, and Regimental Surgeon Gechter, and the Provisions Administrator Ebert, as well as the troops of Lieutenant Colonel von Biesenrodt's Company, and half of the artillery.

2 April - We remained quietly here.

3 April - We raised the anchor and sailed to Dover Castle with a contrary wind. The ship *Betsy* had the misfortune of running against another ship and suffered some damage, and had to remain behind while repairs were made.

4 April - We sailed with a weak wind.

5 April - We arrived in the region of Sheerness, where two ships belonging to our fleet already had dropped anchor.

6 to 13 April - We lay here at anchor. During this time, on 11 April, the agent came to the fleet to us. However, the ship *Betsy* remained behind like *Palliser*, on which Lieutenant Colonel [Friedrich] Platte was to be found, and which had also been damaged. On 12 April *Palliser* and on the following day *Betsy* joined our fleet.

14 April - At six o'clock in the morning, on a signal given by the agent, we raised the anchor and set sail. The wind became contrary at one o'clock in the afternoon and therefore we entered Harwich and awaited a better wind.

15 April - Because of the contrary wind we remained here.

16 April - The wind was rather favorable, so we raised the anchor at six o'clock in the morning and set sail. Toward six o'clock in the evening we had lost sight of land and found ourselves entering the North Sea.

17 and 18 April - We sailed onward until

Journal of the Mirbach Regiment

19 April - when we could see Helgoland so clearly, that because of contrary wind, we had to move away from it and stand out to sea.

20 April - We were fortunate to have a strong wind which enabled us to reach the Weser, where at two o'clock in the afternoon we dropped anchor near Bremerlehe. Here we met the ships of the fleet from Portsmouth, and those regiments had already been transported to Bremen in small boats.

From 21 to 29 April - Until completing the debarkation, the regiments which had previously arrived here had to remain aboard the transport ships.

30 April - At nine o'clock in the morning the regiment was mustered aboard the two ships, *Mary* and *Betsy*. During the afternoon five various size boats came to the ship *Mary*. The troops entered them and were taken to Bremen.

1 May - The small boats approached the ship *Betsy* in order to take the troops on board and then carry them to Bremen.

2 May - About eight o'clock in the morning a part of the regiment arrived in Bremen, while the rest did not arrive until afternoon. We encountered the Hereditary Prince and Prince Charles Regiments aboard their boats. They continued onward on

3 May - in their assigned boats. Today, after eight years, the troops received black bread again, which however, did not taste good to them.

4 and 5 May - We remained in the boats, lying near Bremen.

6 May - The necessary Boecke [small boats] to transport the regiment onward were assigned. At about six o'clock in the afternoon the regiment marched through Bremen with music playing and flags flying and entered the mentioned boats.

7 May - We departed at five o'clock in the afternoon and at eleven o'clock again lay at anchor.

8 May - After raising the anchor, we continued on our voyage at six o'clock in the morning. Before the onset of night, however, we anchored again below the village of Habenhausen.

9 May - At five o'clock in the morning we departed. At eight o'clock we stopped at Dreye, a customs station. The trip originated at Bremen. The many ditches which the horses had to pass, and the many bends in the river, made travel slow. During the afternoon we passed the Achim River, close to which is the small village of the same name. Toward seven o'clock we lay at Usen, which is a village on the left bank. On this side the bank was very high. Here we lost sight of the towers of Bremen. At evening we anchored near the village of Baden.

10 May - At about seven o'clock in the morning our escort from Muenden gave a signal to depart. We had hardly sailed the distance of a rifle shot when the horses had to be transferred across to the right. Here we had covered the three first and the two worst miles [German miles which equal six English miles ?]. Toward eleven o'clock we traveled by the small place called Intschede, a customs station, situated on the right. A half hour later it was noon. At three o'clock, on the left, we saw the mouth of the Aller River and in a short distance the city of Huthbergen on the left, and at eight o'clock Dahlen on the right, and at nine o'clock we discovered Kuen on the left, which is called Koenigsmarck by the sailors.

11 May - We departed at five o'clock in the morning. At eleven o'clock, just one hour below Hoya, we anchored in order to switch the horses, which had been pulling on the left bank, to the right bank. We spent the night in the region of Hoya.

12 May - We arrived at Nienburg at nine o'clock in the evening.

13 May - We anchored at about seven o'clock in the evening near the strong Landesberg, after having passed, a short distance from Liebenau, a dangerous place where many large stones lie in the middle of the river, and the current is very strong.

14 May - We reached the small villages of Doermin and Werden.

15 May - At two-thirty in the evening we anchored a few thousand yards below Minden.

16 May - After we had passed the stone bridge, consisting of nine large and two small arches, with lowered masts, and we progressed very slowly all this day with the help of various farmers pulling the ships instead of horses. Therefore we anchored about nine o'clock near Rehme.

17 May - We arrived at Vetten, and on

18 May - at noon we reached the city of Rinteln. We remained here until on

19 May - at two o'clock in the afternoon, at which time we departed and then anchored at Oldendorf.

Journal of the Mirbach Regiment

20 May - We passed Hameln at eleven o'clock and spent the night in the region of the village of Dorsten.

21 May - We sailed at six o'clock in the morning and after some hours arrived at Gestande, where the ships loaded beer for the soldiers. Also, the horses were transferred from one bank to the other, which required several hours. We then sailed on and anchored at about nine o'clock near Rilican, a Brunswick village.

22 May - Toward three o'clock we passed Holzminden and arrived at Hintern where we anchored at eight o'clock in the evening.

23 May - At six o'clock in the morning we traveled on. Our ship could only reach Herstelle by this evening. The other four sailed to Karlshafen.

24 May - The ship which had stayed at Herstelle sailed at six o'clock in the morning, and in an hour's time reached the others which belonged to the regiment. We then sailed on and anchored at the village of Oedelsheim.

25 May - We dropped anchor at four o'clock in the evening, close to Veckerhagen.

26 May - The regiment arrived at Muenden at two o'clock in the afternoon and on this day the heavy baggage was unloaded.

27 May - The debarkation of the regiment took place at eight o'clock in the morning. We marched through Muenden just after four o'clock, and about eleven o'clock arrived in the capital of our fatherland. We had to wheel onto the parade ground, where His Serene Highness, our dearest prince of the land, inspected us. After this took place, the regiment marched into Bettenhausen.

28 May - The regiment was mustered at the last named place and put on a peacetime footing.

29 May - The regiment moved out and entered quarters at Roehrenfarth and Schwarzburg. However, on the following day,

30 May - the regiment moved into the mentioned Serene Highness' designated stone quarters, where the regiment's grenadier company was already quartered, and is the day when this journal comes to an end.

Journal
of
Lieutenant Rueffer
of
Melsungen

1 March 1776 to 28 December 1777
(To the end of the second campaign, New York)

The von Mirbach Regiment

Translated
by
Bruce E. Burgoyne

Journal
of
Lieutenant Karl Friedrich Rueffer
of Melsungen

- - - - - - -

The Hessian troops which entered the service of the King of Great Britain in 1776 and were sent to America, were the following:

1. Grenadier Battalion von Linsing, formed from the grenadier companies of the 2nd and 3rd Guard Battalions, and the Leib [Body] and von Mirbach Regiments.

2. Grenadier Battalion von Minnigerode, formed from the [grenadier] companies of the Hereditary Prince, Ditfurth, Lossberg, and Knyphausen Regiments.

3. Grenadier Battalion Block, formed from the [grenadier] companies of the Prince Charles, Wutginau, Donop, and Truembach Regiments.

4. Grenadier Battalion Koehler, formed from the [grenadier] companies of the Rall, von Stein, Wissenbach, and Buenau Regiments.

5. Leib Regiment 6. Hereditary Prince 7. Prince Charles 8. Wutginau 9. Ditfurth 10. Donop 11. Lossberg 12. Knyphausen 13. Truembach 14. Mirbach 15. Rall 16. Garrison Regiment Stein 17. Garrison Regiment Wissenbach 18. Garrison Regiment Huyn 19. Garrison Regiment von Buenau, also three companies of artillery, and one company of mounted and four companies of foot jaegers.

The von Mirbach Regiment consisted at the time of departure, like all the other regiments, of five musket and one grenadier company. Each company had four officers, twelve non-commissioned officers, three drummers, one surgeon's assistant, and 105 privates.

The following officers were assigned: 1) Major General [Werner] von Mirbach 2) Colonel [Johann August] von Loos 3) Lieutenant Colonel [Ernst Rudolph] von Schieck 4) Major [Hans Moritz] von Biesenrodt, six captains - [Karl Leopold] Baurmeister, [Louis Marie de] Mallet (grenadier captain), [Johann Wilhelm] Endemann, [Johann Kaspar] Riess, [David] Reichhold, and [Wilhelm Erdmann] von Bogatzky; 1st lieutenants - [Johann Melchior] Rothe (grenadier), and [Friedrich Andreas] Schotten (adjutant-general), 2nd lieutenants - [Johann Ludolph] Rodemann (grenadier), [Johann

Konrad] Riemann, [Karl Friedrich] von Wurmb, [Karl Henrich] von Toll (regimental adjutant), [Dietrich] von Gottschall (grenadier), [Friedrich August] Broescke, [Johann Konrad] Schraidt, and [Ludwig Wilhelm August] von Boyneburg; ensigns - [Karl Friedrich] Rueffer, [Johann Georg] Wiessenmueller, [Hans Friedrich] von Biesenrodt, [Karl Wilhelm] von Bulzingsloewen, and [Ernst] von Drach; middle staff - Regimental Quartermaster [August] Schmidt. Auditor [Johannes] Heinemann, Regimental Surgeon [Karl Konrad] Gechter, and Chaplain [Karl] Eskuche.

First Section
From the departure [from Hesse-Cassel] to the embarkation at Bremerlehe.

1 March - The von Mirbach Regiment marched to Waldau and Crumbach, near Kassel.

2 March - A day of rest. **3 March** - The entire regiment moved to Landwehrhagen.

4 March - The staff and three companies moved to Patterode.

5 March - The staff and two companies moved to Moehringen. The local administrator was Herr von Olderhausen, who extended many courtesies to the staff officers and captains.

6 March - A day of rest. **7 March** - Alfeld was reached by the entire regiment.

8 March - Schulenberg. **9 March** - Rittlingen, where the local administrator and other officials extended courtesies. We passed through Hannover today to the greatest applause, passing in review before Field Marshal Spoerike. Colonel von Loos received a present of a Spanish riding crop with a gold knob.

10 March - A day of rest. **11 March** - Woelpen. **12 March** - Hoya.

13 March - A day of rest. **14 March** - Syke. **15 March** - Massel.

16 March - Osterholz. **17 March** - A day of rest. **18 March** - Hupstedt.

19 March - Otell. **20 March** - Bederkesa, where we rested until the 25th.

26 March - To Schiffdorf, Wulsdorf, and into quarters at Bramel.

28 March - Our regiment was mustered with great ceremony on a meadow near Bremerlehe by the English envoy, Colonel [William] Faucitt, who is a guards officer, and Lieutenant General [Leopold Philipp] von Heister, and met with much approval. **1 April** - The regiment went into quarters at Lehe. It was then embarked. It was a rare view to see such a great fleet for the first time, and to learn of the internal routine of the ship. On the sixteenth, von Heister with his staff embarked aboard the ship *Elizabeth*, which occurred to a continuous cannonade. On the seventeenth, the first fleet sailed, to a constant cannonade, with good weather and a favorable east wind. The fleet carried the regiments: Leib, Hereditary Prince, Prince Charles, Ditfurth, Donop, Lossberg, Truembach, and four companies of the Knyphausen Regiment, the grenadier battalions: von Linsing, von Block, and von Minnigerode; plus one company of jaegers, and consisted of 42 ships. On 19 April our regiment, von Mirbach, embarked on the ships: *Albion, Greyhound, Henry, Union,* and *Eagle*, the last of which also took on the remaining company of the Knyphausen Regiment, Lieutenant [Andreas] Wiederhold, Lieutenant [Johann Friedrich Wilhelm] Briede, Ensign [Wilhelm] von Drach, plus the War Councilor Lorenz and personnel of the commissariat.

Second Section

From the embarkation on the Weser to the debarkation on Staten Island in America.

26 April - About one o'clock during the night, a powerful storm sprang up. At daybreak our captain lowered all the masts, but the wind still rolled the ship so violently that we were in the greatest danger of losing our lives. Toward three o'clock in the afternoon the storm became so strong that we broke our anchorline. The captain put out a second anchor, and as this one also broke, we tried a third one. All was in vain, the last one broke, just as the first one had, and we had to put our trust in the Lord, and at four o'clock in the afternoon we were driven ashore near Geestendorf. From six o'clock until midnight the ship was driven, by frightful pounding, so firmly into the sand, that I can not describe it.

27 April - This morning at ebb tide, our ship stood high and dry on land and we could see clearly how we had been watched over

Ruefer Journal

during yesterday's storm. Not three strides distance lay a stone of tremendous size, and the captain assured us, that we would have foundered without hope of rescue, had we run against it yesterday.

28 April - All the seamen of the entire fleet were engaged in an effort to refloat our ship, but to no avail. Lieutenant Schotten was sent by the general to find out how we were doing. He was able to walk to our ship with dry feet, as the tide was out.

30 April - The occupants of our ship plus provisions and baggage were put aboard other ships as this weight prevented our ship being refloated.

2 May - To our great joy, our ship *Henry* was refloated and this afternoon General von Mirbach again came aboard.

6 May - Once again we were all loaded aboard our ship and received orders at the same time not to allow anyone to leave the ship, as we were to remain ready to sail at anytime.

11 May - Northeast wind, overcast sky, and a cold wind whipping the water. In the morning at nine o'clock a signal shot was fired, that all ships were to get underway. However the wind was contrary and we remained where we were.

12 May - North wind and rainy weather. For us and for all the ship's crew, religious services were held.

(Departure) May 13 - Southwest wind and a bright sky. On the given signal we raised anchor at eight o'clock and departed. We sailed for about one hour and were then compelled to drop anchor in the area of the Danish village of Dettenst, due to a contrary wind.

14 May - Southwest wind and a raw, but bright sky. Two English transport ships arrived.

15 May - West by northwest wind. This morning there was rainy weather. Toward midday the sun came out and the water became choppy. From boredom I began to knit an apron from netting.

16 May - The day began with a strong rain, toward noon was beautiful weather, rather rough.

17 May - Northeast wind and nice weather. Because of a shortage of beer, rum and water were issued today. The water however, was stinking and unpleasant to drink. Therefore it was necessary to mix it in a punch.

18 May - East wind and exceptionally pleasant weather. At three o'clock in the morning the first signal for getting underway was given by means of a cannon shot, at four o'clock the second, immediately after which the event took place. The wind was so advantageous that about eight o'clock, we were able to get off the dangerous sandbar and back into the water and moved into the North Sea. Toward ten o'clock the land was completely out of sight. Most of our people, including all of my cabin mates, became seasick. Our small fleet, consisting of nine ships, and its ever-changing positions, showed us pleasant views during our continuing beautiful weather.

19 May - East wind and pleasant weather. In the afternoon the sun disappeared and with a northeast wind, the sea became rather rough. We traveled eight English miles in one hour.

20 May - East wind and very favorable, only a bit too light. We traveled only three miles in an hour. Toward noon the wind was a little stronger and we attained the speed of yesterday. At five o'clock in the afternoon, on our right we noticed, to our great joy, a church spire, which must have been the outermost English coast of the County of Kent. We also saw the coast of France, near Calais, at five-thirty, then the so-called Cliffs of Dover. An hour before sunset it was possible to see quite clearly the Dover castle in that place. It sat on the side of a high hill about an hour's distance from us and to our right. The city remained hidden from our sight because of the darkness and a heavy fog. In the darkness of the night we saw on our right hand the so-called lighthouse of Dungeness built on a high hill to ensure the safety of the ships.

21 May - Nice weather but rather breezy. Toward eight-thirty we saw the Isle of Wight and a large part of England. The wind slackened gradually and about one o'clock in the afternoon we were lucky enough to anchor in the channel at Portsmouth. We had seen the city from some miles farther out. We arrived too late to see the first fleet because it had already sailed for America on the sixth, with fresh provisions, about 100 sail in number, with eight warships and frigates. This fleet had not been as fortunate on the trip from Lehe here as ours, but had only arrived here on the second.

22 May - Southeast wind and only nice weather. This morning three commissaries were ordered by Admiral Dunclas [Douglas] to visit the unfortunate ship *Henry*. They determined the ship to have been damaged by the grounding in the Weser and that it would be dangerous to use it as a transport for the voyage to America. We were disembarked during the afternoon and reembarked on other ships, the ships *Molly*, *Rockingham* and *Charming Nancy*. I went aboard the *Molly*.

23 May - Southeast wind and beautiful weather, but a very raw day. Because our ship lay at some distance from the others, we raised anchor at six o'clock, sailed to the fleet, and dropped anchor again.

24 May - Southeast wind. The entire fleet moved to a new position not far from the Isle of Wight.

25 May - Southeast wind and generally good weather. This morning at four o'clock a signal was given by our 32-cannon ship *Repulse* for our departure. The anchors were raised and we set sail. Because the wind became too gentle and finally completely died at ten o'clock, on signal we again anchored near the Isle of Wight, which lay to our right. Our fleet consisted now of 26 sail. In the afternoon at four o'clock, on signal, the anchor was again raised and we departed with a southeast wind. Shortly thereafter a special flag and cannon shot signaled us to raise our sails. At six o'clock in the evening a third signal, at which we again, because of contrary winds, returned to our former place and anchored.

26 May - Southwest wind and continued good weather. We departed in the morning, but had hardly sailed as far as on the first day, when because of an exceptional calm, we were again given a signal to anchor, and we remained still until four o'clock. The frigate, despite contrary winds, gave the signal to depart. We tacked for an hour and the frigate gave a fifth signal to return. As night fell the frigate gave a sixth signal for us to depart again.

27 May - West-southwest wind and good weather. We believed by daybreak we would have lost sight of the Isle of Wight, but became aware that during the night we had traveled only a few miles, as we could still see the whole island. The exceptional calm had nearly prevented the ship from moving from its position, so that finally Captain Davis, that was the frigate commander's name, found it necessary at four o'clock in the afternoon to give the signal to anchor, whereupon the ships, to reduce the nearly imperceptible movement, dropped a small anchor. About two hours later the signal was given again to raise the anchor, which was done at once, but to little purpose. All these unsuccessful attempts to sail made us understand quite clearly that the commander must have been given very strict

Rueffer Journal

orders for our most expeditious departure and arrival in America. Because of a shortage of coffee, today we had to begin the sorry practice of only drinking it once a day. I knit diligently on the netting to somewhat reduce my brooding over the coffee.

28 May - West-northwest wind. Now it appears we have begun our trip in an orderly manner, because we can no longer see land. We met a ship from America today, which said that it had seen our fleet, about 150 sail strong (because 42 ships had joined from Scotland) fourteen days ago. In the afternoon we saw the coast by Portland. The wind became contrary and very violent, especially during the night. It meant tacking, the sails were mostly lowered, and the sky was very dark.

29 May - South wind and still very violent. The sky was very bright. It was still necessary to tack constantly and the strong wind caused many people to get sick. About four o'clock in the afternoon we saw the harbor of Plymouth on our right at a distance of about twenty miles. The wind grew even more violent. The constant tacking made our remaining in the cabin not only impossible but also unbearable. About midnight the strong wind changed into a very violent storm. Everything that was not securely fastened crashed noisily about the cabin.

30 May - South wind and still as strong as ever, and rain. All but the two middle-most sails were taken in. The fleet is completely scattered, only six ships still being visible to the straining eyes. The storm was so strong that we could not cook. My associates (five) in the cabin were sick, but I ate a piece of cold chicken, because thank God, I am healthy. At six o'clock in the evening the sky cleared somewhat and the wind began to blow a bit easier and we were able to sleep more peacefully this night than on the previous one.

31 May - South-southwest wind and still not favorable. The sky is bright, and as the storm is no longer so strong, six ships of the fleet have gathered together, including the *Albion*. Three more rejoined the fleet this afternoon. At four o'clock we caught sight of the distant coast of England. The harbor at Falmouth lies about twenty miles to our right.

1 June - Southwest wind but barely noticeable. We spent a peaceful night. Three ships are still missing. Toward noon the wind picked up and we sailed rather well. At two o'clock our still missing ships joined up. We met a Holland warship which saluted our fleet with five cannon shots. The salute was acknowledged in return with nine cannon shots.

2 June - North wind and generally fair weather. The night was calm. Although the wind is somewhat stronger, as well as steady, our ship appears to remain motionless. This afternoon the wind became contrary, but improved again toward evening.

3 June - North wind and strong, but good weather. All the ships sailed well and we traveled four English miles an hour. During the afternoon the wind raged a great deal and was accompanied by rain. Toward evening the sky cleared again.

4 June - North-northwest wind with a dark sky and very strong. The constantly rolling waves washed over the ship and we traveled six or seven miles an hour. We heard from our captain the welcome assurance that with this wind we could be in America in four weeks, but during the night it became weaker.

5 June - West by northwest wind, a dark sky, and a warm day with some rain. Toward evening the sky brightened.

6 June - West wind and bright sunshine, but also very rough. The night was spent most unpleasantly. We traveled only fifty minutes in an hour. It was nearly impossible to remain in the cabin except in bed.

7 June - North-northwest wind and nice weather. Most of the people who had been seasick were now recovered.

8 June - North-northwest wind, rather strong with an unpleasant fog and rainy. Toward noon a bit more pleasant.

9 June - Northwest wind, a real summer day. As there is no foliage to be seen, it is necessary for us to seek shade from the too hot sun under the sails. A signal at nine o'clock called a meeting of ships' captains on board the frigate in order to receive orders. Therefore we remained standing nearly still in one place the entire day. We learned from our captain that apparently we were to debark at Halifax. At seven o'clock we departed again. In the twilight the sky looked very dull.

10 June - Northwest wind and a bright sky although very stormy since midnight. The storm grew steadily stronger. By mealtime a comical situation had arisen. No dishes or plates stood on the table. Everyone who wished to eat anything, had to eat from a plate, held in his hand, while swaying back and forth. Toward evening the captain informed us that we had reached the Bay of Biscay. The waves beat high as a house-top. The tallest masts had to be lowered. This storm did not seem strange to us. This sea is very rough, more so than all others, but above all, we were not concerned. What had been unusual before, became ordinary.

11 June - Northwest wind and clear weather. The night was spent most unpleasantly. It was necessary to tie oneself in bed in order to prevent falling out. The storm just would not let up.

12 June - West-southwest wind with rainy weather and a rather calm sea. As we had passed the Bay of Biscay and had reached a part of the Portuguese Sea we could easily notice the difference between the two. We traveled at about four to five miles an hour. We were, according to the captain's reckoning, about 450 miles from Portsmouth.

13 June - West wind and clear weather, toward afternoon, dull and rainy. We heard 22 cannon shots during the night. All the ships were required immediately to hang lanterns at the stern and to draw closer together. It was something completely out of the ordinary and we could not guess the reason, which is still unknown to us. We believed it to be because some enemy ships were in the area. At four o'clock in the afternoon an innumerable amount of fish, which the English call porpoise, appeared near our ship. Our ship's quartermaster caught one with a harpoon and we discovered that it looks more like a swine than like a fish. [The German word for porpoise is Meerschwein which translated literally means sea pig.]

14 June - Southwest wind, rainy, and stormy. Today we reached the Sea of Biscay, which is also very rough. The captain assured us that the storms would no longer be so violent, because we were past the worst seas.

15 June - Southwest wind and fair weather, and although the waves were very high, still there was no storm. It was so foggy that we could not see the ships that were only a short distance from us.

16 June - North wind but nevertheless not a good wind for sailing. We were very melancholy as the ship nearly stood still and the wind was almost unnoticeable. Toward evening it increased and we sailed on in a lightly falling rain.

17 June - West-southwest wind and rainy. We slept peacefully this night. We traveled along the desired course at two to three miles per hour.

18 June - North-northeast wind and the best sailing wind. Sunny and very pleasant weather. The wind only a bit too light. We traveled one and one-half miles per hour. Today we learned the significance of the cannon fire on the night of the thirteenth. The ship *Gobarth*, which had provisions on board, rammed the *Albion*, not only knocking down the jack mast, but doing such great harm that the ship took on much water, and because it was believed on the ship that it would founder, they had fired the signal for help.

19 June - North-northeast wind and because it is very calm with beautiful weather, we travel, with this exceptionally good wind, four to six miles in one hour. It was cloudy and a pleasant day. We were guests of the captain for the second time, and this time our excellently prepared meal was fully enjoyed. The owner of the ship receives 150 pounds sterling from the King each month, but must pay and feed the captain and the crew.

20 June - North-northwest wind. We maintained our course today but because the wind was contrary, we traveled only two miles per hour. Toward evening it became very foggy.

21 June - North wind and very favorable. A very pleasant day. We traveled at five miles per hour and the captain assured us that we could travel at nine miles per hour, if we were not held back by slower ships, which often caused us to shorten sails.

22 June - East-northeast wind with beautiful weather. In general, a favorable wind with very calm water. Because our ship wandered off station, we received a warning shot from the frigate to get back and stay on the right station. The captain must pay one pound sterling for each warning shot received, and if he does not heed the first one, then a second, third, and so on is given, doubled each time and the money goes to support the mariners' hospital.

23 June - East-southeast wind, strong and gusty. We traveled eight miles an hour. The water was, by beautiful weather, very rough from twelve o'clock yesterday until today, and in this time we traveled 133 miles. Because of a shortage of beer, today began the sad initiation of using rum and water. Now we wish more strongly than before to reach our destination. We seek to alleviate the greatest thirst by mixing it in punch and other drinks because the water stinks and is nearly impossible to drink, but this is not possible either, for fear daily of the greatest sorrow, running out of sugar for our coffee.

24 June - North-northeast wind and an overcast sky. The wind very favorable. We traveled 150 miles in 24 hours. Toward noon we saw to the north the Spanish Azores' island of St. Michael. Because we changed course we hoped we would take on fresh water.

25 June - Northeast wind, and beautiful weather. Five or six miles per hour.

26 June - North-northeast wind, the beautiful weather of yesterday. We did not travel as well however. This night the wind blew so strong that we feared a storm. However it soon calmed. Today a turtle or sea tortoise came close to our ship. It was about as large as a medium size table. Towards evening, rain.

27 June - South wind and pleasantly warm, but very annoying. There was nearly no wind blowing. Calm. As to the hope of stopping at St. Michael, we quietly put the idea to bed.

28 June - South wind and beautiful weather. At a given signal all the ships had to send a report to Lieutenant Talmain on the *Albion*. We still believed we would sail to St. Michael, and Lieutenant von Wurmb therefore, with this fond hope, made coffee even before I left my bed. I acted the good companion and excused his zeal as it was still uncertain that we would stop there. This still was not enough. His wastefulness, resulting from the joy of soon being able to buy fresh provisions, was carried to the point that without my consent, he had one of the steers slaughtered and this had no sooner happened than he wished it were still alive, because the captain brought the news back that we would not be stopping here. Several staff officers were invited aboard the frigate for the noon meal, and so we learned from the lieutenant colonel that it was the commander's opinion that we would debark at New York. Even he was still not certain however, as he would only be permitted to open his sealed orders when we reached a certain location. According to the commander's calculations we had not yet completed half of our journey, being only 1,400 miles distant from Portsmouth and therefore he had ordered that the water be used sparingly. Captain Reiss of our regiment is very sick and probably will not live another fortnight.

Rueffer Journal

29 June - West by southwest wind, but very light with beautiful weather.

30 June - The same. Today, for the first time, we had to forgo coffee. Toward three o'clock we saw the three Azores Islands of St. George, St. Pico, and St. Taracern.

1 July - West to southwest wind with rainy, stormy weather.

2 July - North wind, very good for sailing. The frigate, by means of nine cannon shots, signaled that during the night the ships, even during high wind, should remain as close together as possible so that they would not become scattered too easily.

3 July - Northwest wind and beautiful weather. Toward evening the sky became overcast.

4 July - West wind and completely contrary with rain. We spent nearly the entire night tacking, first to the south, then to the north. Toward evening stormy.

5 July - West wind and since five this morning, very good sailing. A hot day. Toward noon, calm.

6 July - This was also a sad day. My tobacco twist ran out and unfortunately my supply of snuff and sugar will soon be exhausted.

7 July - North wind and beautiful weather, and nearly the same calm. Toward evening a south by southeast wind and a bit stronger, so that we made some progress.

8 July - South by southwest wind, beautiful but unbearably hot. Two or three miles [per hour ?].

9 July - South by southwest wind, but we tacked many miles.

10 July - West wind and still beautiful weather, continued tacking. The water was very rough. Toward evening however, rather calm again.

11 July - Southwest wind and a completely calm sea, impossibly hot. Because the frigate was short of water, we and all the ships had to give up two casks of water. Because of a shortage of sugar, which ran out today, everyone had to give up warm drinks.

12 July - West wind and continued beautiful weather, but against a contrary wind we sailed only two miles. Today Lieutenant von Wurmb and I celebrated the saint's day for people named Henrich and Henrietta, with considerable pleasure. The health and long life of all our dear friends of these names were toasted by us, frequently, with the only bottle of red wine and a bottle of white wine. Toward evening our soldiers entertained with dancing on deck, and we were moved to do the same, but unfortunately without the company of women.

13 July - West wind and still continued beautiful weather. We tacked nearly the entire day. Today we saw flying fish for the first time.

14 July - North by northwest wind and the same weather as yesterday. We sailed quite well today. Toward evening a northeast wind.

15 July - Southwest wind, but so light that we could barely detect any movement. Toward noon the wind increased so that we at least made some progress.

16 July - North wind and calm. The sea was like yesterday, but we moved ahead a bit. The sailors held a christening today for those who had not previously been to America. They put blindfolds on them, used fat and lampblack to blacken their faces, and then those with black faces were shaved so closely with a wood rasp that afterwards the blood flowed. Next they were dunked in barrels of water as if being baptized.

18 July - East by northeast wind and still beautiful weather, but the wind was of no value as it hardly blew at all. With the last steer and the last wine, today we begin the saint's day of Lieutenant Wurmb's sweet Karoline. We occupied our time very well according to the custom aboard ship. Our captain received visitors from other ships today and we were his guests.

19 July - South wind and beautiful weather. We sailed well. Our ship's crew caught a ravenous fish, ten feet long and weighing 170 pounds, a shark.

20 July - South wind and again, beautiful weather.

21 July - The same weather. There was a very sad event today. A soldier named [Hermann] Dietz, of the Lieutenant Colonel's Company, has been missing since two o'clock this morning. We believed that he had hidden himself in the hold of the ship for fear of the punishment he was to have received this morning, having committed a theft, but to our greatest wonder, after thoroughly searching everywhere, he was not to be found, so that no other thought remained except that through intent or carelessness, he had fallen overboard. Toward noon a strange ship was seen to the south and the frigate sailed toward it at once. At the same time a second one appeared to the north, toward which Lieutenant Talmain sailed. During the evening the frigate returned to the fleet and we learned that the ship was a Portuguese from Brazil bound for Lisbon. The latter however, was a merchant ship loaded with rockfish from America from Tarenouse and heading for the West Indies. It was also learned that General [William] Howe had taken his army into the port of Halifax and that the troops had been forced to leave Boston. At the same time we learned that they could give us no news of our first fleet.

22 July - South wind and beautiful weather, six miles per hour.

23 July - West by southwest wind and rather overcast. About eight o'clock this morning it became north by northeast and beautiful weather. Six or seven miles per hour. The frigate signaled that each transport ship should provide a guard force of one officer and twenty privates under orders of General von Mirbach, a sign that we would soon reach the American coast.

25 July - East by northeast wind, but gentle, fine weather. Toward afternoon, south-southeast wind, five miles.

26 July - South-southwest wind and fine weather. A flying fish landed on deck today. It was sky-blue on its back and white on its belly. It had four fins like fine gauze.

27 July - South wind, bright but very stormy. We sailed rapidly.

28 July - West wind and still very stormy. At four o'clock in the afternoon the storm became more violent and was accompanied by lightning. We had to lower all but the middle-most sails. The wind switched to the northwest.

29 July - Northeast and beautiful weather. If only we had not been forced to lower nearly all the sails because of the slower ships, we could have covered many miles today.

30 July - Southeast wind, but very weak. Fine weather. Calm. Today we received some fresh provisions. Lieutenant von Wurmb went to the *Eagle* and purchased not only sugar and tobacco, but also two flagons of red wine and a pound of coffee.

1 August - West wind and very stormy weather. An individual soon gets so vexed and impatient because of contrary winds, that he would rather die than remain at sea. There was an eclipse of the moon tonight, four hours earlier than indicated in the Hessian almanac. During our unpleasantly prolonged journey we have experienced many storms, but none more violent than today's. During our noon meal a wave crashed through the cabin window and swamped Lieutenant Wurmb's bed. Toward evening the storm abated and the wind swung to the north and later to the northeast.

2 August - Northeast wind and very favorable, but because yesterday's storm had damaged many ships, all sails were lowered. We hope for land in eight days.

3 August - Southeast wind and fine weather. Until ten o'clock the sea was calm as a pond, then the wind came up and we sailed swiftly. This evening a storm with lots of lightning, but little thunder.

4 August - Southeast wind and with fine weather, a calm sea. Toward twelve o'clock the wind began to blow well, six or seven miles per hour. We caught many fish.

5 August - Southeast wind and beautiful weather. From noon yesterday until noon today, we sailed 128 miles along the desire course. We met a ship, a packetboat, which had arrived here from London in 37 days. The ship had 22 cannons. We were sure that the missing soldier, Dietz, had drowned on 21 July, so that it was unexpected, when at ten o'clock our Quartermaster Canade found him when Dietz asked for some water. He was immediately brought on deck and admitted stealing things since our voyage began. He had also nourished himself during his desertion by theft and had been in the ship's supplies as well as on deck every night in order to get something to drink. The lieutenant colonel feared he would now do what we thought he had done. Therefore he was locked up and watched with a guard. He had grown so weak and miserable under the casks in the ship, where he had hidden, that a person could not approach him without his fainting.

6 August - Southeast wind and again beautiful weather. We hope soon to escape the violent elements.

7 August - Southeast wind and the same good weather. If the wind continues in this manner, we hope soon to see land.

8 August - Southeast wind and the beautiful weather which we had become really accustomed to expect. The ocean water no longer looks so blue and green, but more brown because of the shallower depth.

9 August - Southwest wind and a completely calm sea which again eliminates our hope of landing soon. We learned that we are to debark at New York. A packetboat had been sent from London for that purpose and to discover why no report had yet been received of the first fleet.

10 August - Northeast wind and still a calm sea, later stronger wind, four miles per hour. We tell ourselves that we will see land by day after tomorrow. Because of this longing we can hardly sleep.

11 August - Northeast wind and pleasant weather. At three o'clock this morning we cast the lead for the first time, found 45 fathoms, and there is no doubt that we will soon reach our destination. We met three ships, English provisions ships, and the frigate *Perseus*, which had neither heard nor seen anything of our first fleet.

12 August - East wind. The frigate signaled with four cannon shots and a lantern at the mast for the ships to lower sails and tie their rudders fast because land was near and we would wait here until daybreak. When it was barely light we could clearly see the coast of America, especially Sandy Hook. To all appearances it seemed very pleasant. By full daylight we could see a number of ships to the north and we assumed them to be the first or third fleet. It was the first fleet which had an unfortunately long voyage. There are regiments in it which have been on board since 23 March. The frigate sailed at six o'clock. About one o'clock in the afternoon we passed between Sandy Hook, where for the safety of shipping a lighthouse has been built, and Long Island, sailed past the dangerous sandbanks, past half of the fleet, and finally, the pleasant view, more than twenty warships and frigates and 400 transports lay at anchor before Staten Island and New York. New York was still held by the rebels. General [William] Howe with 20,000 men was already in camp on Staten Island, opposite New York. This island is about ten miles long and three miles wide, and the only one in this province occupied by the King of England. We were on board the ships sixteen weeks and five days, and had been at sea from Portsmouth eleven weeks and three days. The night was very pleasant. All the ships had lanterns and this made a beautiful illumination.

13 August - Everything was peaceful in the fleet. During a storm at Whitsuntide many of the ships had been scattered, forcing them to enter Halifax, which the entire fleet also did. [The ship of] Captain [Peter Michael] Waldenberg of the Leib Regiment was also separated [from the fleet] and during that time, without a shot, captured as a prize an American ship. Lieutenant [Karl August] Kleinschmidt and Captain [Simon Ludwig Wilhelm] Count von der Lippe, both of the Leib Regiment, had an unfortunate duel and the count died of his wounds to the body the following day. Today General von Heister made his visit to the commanding general, Howe, and was saluted by cannons from all the warships as he passed.

14 August - We still do not know when we will debark. Today I was on land for the first time and had almost forgotten how to walk, or more correctly, I was no longer accustomed to it. We bought fresh fish and coffee, which we had been without for so long. Von Heister and all the generals were guests of General Howe.

Rueffer Journal

Third Section

From the debarkation in America at Staten Island for the first campaign until entering winter quarters in New York.

15 August - This morning at five o'clock we received orders to debark immediately, which followed at once amidst considerable confusion. There was a lot of commotion. Ship's provisions for two days were carried, but we had to leave most of our equipment on the ship. It was night before we had set up camp. English headquarters is at Richmond.

16 August - Today all the regimental commanders had to go to the Hessian headquarters, which is near our camp. The most diligent training was ordered. Our life style is not the best as we have received no money. Officers as well as privates have had to live on ship's provisions. The climate and the area in general are not much different from ours. The order was sent out today that the entire officer corps was to cut all silver from their uniforms so as to appear as nearly as possible like common soldiers because the rebels are excellent shots and at every opportunity draw a bead on the officers. Long Island, which lies opposite our camp, is full of rebels and their activity is clearly visible.

17 August - As the cartridges which we brought from Hesse are mostly spoiled, we have turned ours in and each man has received sixty new ones, but the younger recruits waste the powder.

18 August- There was a strong exchange of cannon fire this morning in the harbor at New York between three English and four American frigates. The first wished to reconnoiter the harbor and apparently they did very little harm. The Hessian Grenadiers and Jaegers and four English regiments received orders today to be transferred over to Long Island. About eight o'clock however, because of the incessant rain, they were ordered back.

19 August - Today nine English battalions were embarked. The brigade of General Stirn occupied their camp, as it was feared the rebels in New Jersey would make a descent against us because the water near this place was very shallow.

20 August - Nothing new (and this is the case when a date is skipped).

21 August - All the Hessian Grenadiers and one company of Jaegers embarked today in order to approach the shore of Long Island tonight, thus making the attack that much easier tomorrow morning. General [Charles, Earl] Cornwallis commands the entire operation. Instead of bread today, we received flour. We had such a strong storm today that no one can remember ever having experienced a stronger one.

22 August - This morning at nine o'clock the English who had embarked on the nineteenth, as well as our grenadiers, who were embarked yesterday, landed on Long Island without meeting any resistance. We wish and hope to follow soon. The strength of this corps is 15,000 men.

23 August - We still remain quietly here. On the other hand, our grenadiers and jaegers on Long Island have small skirmishes daily. Still the enemy every time gets the worst of it.

24 August - We changed our camp today and are again in battalion formation. In another skirmish on Long Island today the worthy Colonel [Karl Emil Ulrich von] Donop was in danger of being shot by an enemy sharpshooter, or as they are called, rifleman. By the greatest good fortune when the rebel met him, the rebel's weapon misfired, so the colonel took his weapon and shot him through the head. [It is not clear whose weapon was used by the colonel.] Major [Georg Henrich] Pauli of the Artillery and Lieutenant von Donop, adjutant to Colonel von Donop, were both slightly wounded. One jaeger was killed and five wounded, and ten grenadiers were wounded.

25 August - At twelve o'clock tonight the Stirn and Mirbach Brigades, the first consisting of the Lossberg, Knyphausen, and Rall Regiments, the latter of the Hereditary Prince, Donop, and Mirbach Regiments, received orders to be ready by the water at eleven o'clock to be transferred across to

Long Island. As soon as we landed on that side and assembled, we began our march. Toward evening we joined Cornwallis' corps and moved into camp at Gravesend, where the Hessian headquarters were set up. We found this corps had very little concealment. About 100 yards from our front was a thick forest in which many rebels were lurking. We had been allowed to take nothing but tents and the most necessary items from our baggage. Everything else was left aboard ship. The Lossberg Brigade, consisting of the Leib, Prince Charles, Ditfurth, and Truembach Regiments, remained on Staten Island. We passed through a pleasant region, now and again country homes which had been completely destroyed. This island is about 160 miles long and in many places 25 miles wide, very fertile and pleasant.

26 August - We moved a few miles to the settlement of Flatbush. Lieutenant Schraidt and I were ordered to cover the riflemen and a short distance ahead could vaguely see the rebels. A picket of the 71st Scottish Regiment was constantly engaged with the enemy close by my post.

27 August - Our detachments and pickets were engaged with the rebels the entire night. As day broke the grenadiers moved out of their camp to make the first serious assault. It was not long before the firing increased. Toward eight o'clock General von Heister came and ordered the Stirn and Mirbach Brigades to break camp at once, which was done. Adjutant Lieutenant Marquard withdrew the Hereditary Prince Regiment in order to advance it toward the von Minnigerode Grenadier Battalion. Donop [Regiment] won a height in its front without meeting resistance. The Mirbach Brigade, which General [Johann Daniel] Stirn commands since yesterday, and which includes the Lossberg, Knyphausen, and Rall Regiments, for the most part covered our left flank. Our regiment advanced on the height with Donop on our left. As soon as we reached this point, the enemy opened fire on us with small arms from the woods. As nothing was to be accomplished however, because of the great protection afforded the entire [enemy] battalion,

Lieutenant Schraidt and I were sent into the thicket with some eighty flankers, which resulted in each of us taking some captives in a distance of only about fifteen yards. The enemy were hidden in the thickest bushes and no one could have known where they were if they had not made their presence known by firing on their opponents. They were all so fearful and would almost rather be shot dead than surrender, because their generals and other officers had told them they would be hanged. Because our drive had such success, we continued the push until after dark and the detachment led by Lieutenant Schraidt and me captured 61 prisoners, including eleven officers. I was fortunate enough to capture a horse with a saddle and bridle, which according to our captives, had belonged to a Colonel Kiglain of the sharpshooters, who had been shot dead. They could not have been taken for soldiers as they had no uniforms, but only torn blouses of all colors; no similar weapons, but one had a musket while another was armed with a rifle. Our entire corps bivouacked this night.

28 August - This morning at daybreak we were again sent into the woods with our flankers of yesterday, to seek out those rebels still in hiding. We only found 23 men. Toward nine o'clock we returned to camp, received orders to make a charge, and marched about two miles farther, where we again had the rebels very close to our front and were only separated from them by a swamp. During yesterday's affair the rebels lost two generals, [John] Sullivan and [William Alexander, Lord] Stirling, 35 other officers, and 485 men, all of whom were captured alive.

29 August - The prisoners were under guard at the village of Flatbush. Occasionally each side fired its cannons and as soon as the heavy artillery arrives, it will be necessary for the enemy to move out of their camp.

30 August - This night the enemy evacuated all its camps and even all of Long Island, which no one had expected, as only yesterday they had set up a strong battery, of which eleven cannons were abandoned.

Rueffer Journal

31 August - Today we changed camps and moved to Brooklyn Ferry in the area directly opposite New York, which the enemy still occupies, and immediately manned both defensive positions at Brooklyn and Red Hook. The Hessian headquarters was at Brooklyn.

2 September - This night the rebels on New York fired several times at our position, however without the least effect.

3 September - The English headquarters is at Newtown.

5 September - This evening at the change of the watch on the heights, the enemy fired several cannon shots, but without evil consequences. General von Heister received orders to direct a counter-fire with two 12-pounders and tomorrow these will probably silence the enemy's cannons.

7 September - The rebels attacked a warship which was lying near New York, tonight. Nine cannon shots drove them off before they could accomplish anything.

8 September - Today we heard that our right wing, where the English are, with the help of a warship, repulsed an attack without loss to our side.

9 September - Today we learned that the enemy is building a strong battery.

10 and 11 September - We spent these two days working diligently on fortifications.

12 September - As our battery was finished, we fired a few rounds at the enemy. Our brigade received orders to be ready to march at a moment's notice.

13 September - Three frigates passed New York on the East River today and dropped anchor off our right wing. They received, but did not reply to a heavy cannonade. Our batteries on the other hand, fired all the heavier. We received information about an attack against the enemy to be launched in a few days, and were commended by the commander-in-chief for our probe into the woods on 27 August.

Rueffer Journal

14 September - This evening we received orders to march tomorrow morning at two-thirty. Today another three warships passed into the East River and anchored by yesterday's ships.

15 September - Yesterday's orders were put into effect today. At three o'clock everyone was under arms and we marched off from the left. About six o'clock General [James] Grant's Division, to which our brigade belongs, halted. A short time later a strong firing of both cannons and small arms was to be heard, which was our warships firing at the enemy shore. General [Henry] Clinton then moved his first division, consisting of the Mountain Scots, the Light Infantry, the Hessian Grenadiers, the English Grenadiers, and the Hessian Jaegers, into flatboats which were ready on the shore and made his attack, whereupon the second division immediately followed and landed at Purtee Bay on New York Island, fortunately without the least resistance. The enemy had fled from all his positions and this prevented our making many captives. Because of a language misunderstanding the Grenadier Company of the Wutginau Regiment suffered one man killed and eleven wounded because Captain [Friedrich von] Eschwege attacked a troop which wished to lay down its arms. Because he did not understand and continued to advance, the enemy kept their weapons and kept firing during their retreat. Because we had left our baggage behind, we spent the night behind the Grenadiers, without our tents. The Mirbach Brigade remained on Long Island.

16 September - According to reports of deserters, the rebels lost 186 men. The English Light Infantry and Jaegers were heavily engaged again yesterday, with the enemy getting the short end of the stick, although the English took many casualties. The enemy has completely abandoned New York and all of them have fled into Fort Washington, which lies on the point of this island, near Connecticut, and in a very strongly fortified position.

17 September - The entire corps was commended today for the successful attack.

18 September - This morning we moved into a regular camp behind the Grenadiers, which are behind the Johns house. The area is called Blumenthal [Bloomingdale].

20 September - Because of the carelessness of the outposts, the arrival of thirty deserters caused the regiment to be alerted.

21 September - There was a great fire behind our front at twelve o'clock tonight, which we assumed to come from New York, and which we found to be the case as soon as it was light. About 100 rebels who had remained hidden in the empty houses and cellars set the fire and even though the English garrison, which consisted of three battalions, turned out at once, two churches and 400 houses to windward were laid in ashes. One of those criminals was thrown in the fire, another hanged by the legs and burned.

22 September - At twelve o'clock at night we received orders to be ready to march, along with eight English battalions, at nine o'clock. This was carried out at twelve o'clock. We marched to the North River in order to be transported across to Paulus Hook in New Jersey. The wind was so contrary that the warships which were to cover the movement of the flatboats from land could not get into position. Therefore, at five o'clock we returned to our camp. Today an enemy spy was captured near the English artillery park. [Nathan Hale ?]

23 September - This afternoon at four o'clock eight English battalions captured the fort at Paulus Hook from the rebels. The landing was carried out very fortunately because the wind was favorable for the warships. It is an important position, very advantageous for us. The debarkation in New Jersey was thus covered. The rebels conducted themselves very poorly.

24 September - This morning the brigade of General Stirn was mustered by Colonel Charles Osborn and received many commendations.

2 October - After remaining peacefully in camp for such a long time, the Stirn Brigade camp was changed today. It marched half an hour forward and took position behind the Grenadiers' fortifications. Here we held the most advanced posts. The enemy outposts were about 200 yards from us.

3 to 8 October - Nothing new. Our outposts were occasionally alarmed by the rebels, but never so heavily that the regiment had to fall out.

9 October - This morning at eight o'clock two warships, two frigates, and a bomb galley sailed up the North River to Kingsbridge. They received a heavy cannonade from the enemy batteries on both sides of the river, but no harm was done. Toward eleven o'clock the firing ceased. At one o'clock in the afternoon a heavy cannonade was again heard, but at a great distance. It appeared the warships had taken their positions and now were firing upon the enemy batteries. According to confirmed reports they captured three enemy three-masted ships and forty boats.

11 October - Tonight at eleven o'clock nearly all the English as well as the Hessian Grenadiers and Jaegers marched, even the Leib Regiment and the Prince Charles and Ditfurth Regiments, which until now have remained on Staten Island, and even the Lossberg, Knyphausen, and Rall Regiments, which were on Long Island. The English and Donop Brigades were landed on the East River and all the listed regiments landed at Rockport in Connecticut, a peninsula considered part of New York. General von Heister went with this corps. Here in Blumenthal four English regiments and the Stirn Brigade remain under the command of [Hugh] Lord Percy.

15 October - Nothing is heard from General Howe who is with the corps in Connecticut. Reports from New England put General [John] Burgoyne nearby.

17 October - Today we heard a passing report that on the thirteenth, at Winchester, General Howe wished to attack the rebels, but they were so numerous that no attack had been launched and the force returned to camp.

18 October - Today our third fleet dropped anchor between Staten and Long Islands. It contained the Wutginau Regiment, Koehler Grenadier Battalion, and the four garrison regiments of von Stein, von Wissenbach, von Huyn, and von Buenau, as well as one company of Jaegers, one company of Artillery, and a Waldeck regiment. General [Wilhelm, Freiherr von] Knyphausen and Major General [Martin] Schmidt are with this fleet.

19 October - Today an enemy deserter reported that in Fort Washington and all its outworks on this island there are only 4,000 men.

21 October - Today it was learned that General [Charles] Lee had nearly been captured.

24 October - Today we received orders to be ready to move out. The regiment was to make a reconnaissance of the enemy camps, but the order was countermanded.

25 October - It was reported that on the 23rd, the third fleet passed up the East River in flatboats and landed at Frog Neck and encamped near New Rochelle.

27 October - I was ordered on command. Lieutenant Colonel von Schieck, as staff officer of the day, sent out a patrol to reconnoiter the enemy's outposts. I had not gone far before encountering them and then returned to where we met the Donop Regiment, which together with six English battalions, had been ordered to launch a false attack on the enemy lines and Fort Washington so that General von Knyphausen could more easily approach Kingsbridge and the above mentioned fort. Our regiment provided cover for the camp. During the attack, General Johns [Valentine Jones] commanded the right wing and Colonel [Karl Wilhelm] von Hackenberg the left wing. The English suffered four men killed and three lightly wounded; the enemy's losses are unknown, but greater than ours.

28 October - The regiments which had moved forward remained there until nine o'clock this evening, when they returned to their camp without being disturbed by the enemy. General von Knyphausen supposedly has suffered greater losses at Kingsbridge than the rebels.

30 October - General Grant's English Brigade marched to join the main army. Therefore our camp was changed.

31 October - We learned of a reconnaissance made by General [Sir William] Erskine with the Ewald Jaeger Company and the Rall Regiment. The results are still unknown, however.

1 November - This evening we received a report that 300 riflemen had come from Jersey to launch an attack. Therefore, all the reserve pickets were called out.

2 November - We rested easily this night. This morning we heard a heavy cannonade toward Kingsbridge. The following announcement was received from White Plains:

Announcement from the Adjutant General

His Excellence, Lieutenant General von Heister, Captain Baurmeister, dated 31 October 1776

"On the 24th of this month we marched from York's Continent to Chester, where the Philipse's men live, and on the 28th to this place, where we encountered the enemy at the start of the While Plain, and battled against them from one height to the next for an hour and one-half until he crawled back into his fortified camp and darkness settled over the clash. The Lossberg Regiment performed miracles. My general, Lieutenant Werner, and I were caught in such a hail of bullets that the dragoon orderly was wounded and Lieutenant Werner's horse was shot in the flank. This fire lasted only eight minutes until the Rall Regiment helped the Lossberg Regiment out of the tight situation with a general discharge, formed in line in the best of order, and captured the height. Lossberg, whose left wing had to wade up to the waist and then had to move through a burned out woods, suffered thirteen men wounded. Captain [Friedrich Wilhelm] von Benning and a standard bearer, [Free Corporal Georg Henrich] Kress nearly drowned. Free Corporal [Gottlieb] Waldeck had the colors shot out of his hand and the flag flew in such a manner that it was a joy to see. The field pieces of the Lossberg, Knyphausen, and Rall Regiments began such a racket that it became impossible to hear or see, but the enemy withdrew so quickly that there was little effect to be noted from the cannonade. A discharge from the Knyphausen Regiment struck a rebel regiment so solidly that it wounded 92 men. The English 49th Regiment which followed Lossberg also suffered a great many casualties."

Now we are face to face with the enemy. The Knyphausen corps on the 24th followed our march with the two regiments, Huyn and Wissenbach. The rest remained at Rochelle where the corps landed on the 22nd and the same day, Captain Ewald's Jaeger Company, which had just gotten on land, made an attack near Miles Square, which was not successful. The enemy stood fast and Ewald had two men killed, Lieutenant [Karl] von Rau and two jaegers wounded, and two men missing. However, on the 26, when General Erskine with Ewald's Jaegers, the Rall Regiment, and a squadron of light dragoons was on reconnaissance beyond Miles Square, Ewald got his two captured jaegers back, captured 19 men, and destroyed a magazine for rum and flour. Now the Knyphausen Regiment has marched, day before yesterday, toward Kingsbridge and yesterday occupied the enemy works on this side. The enemy still occupies Fort Washington and likewise Fort Constitution in New Jersey. The enemy is now moving toward Boston with all heavy equipment. General Burgoyne defeated the rebels this side of Albany on 2 October and secured that area.

3 November - We received reports that the enemy had been driven from their trenches the other side of Kingsbridge, having left many cannons behind. Today two transport ships which have provisions for General Burgoyne dropped anchor in the North River.

5 November - These ships sailed with a frigate escort. They received a heavy fire from the enemy batteries in New Jersey, but suffered no damage.

[??] - Today we received information that General Knyphausen had actually captured Kingsbridge and is in possession of it. This evening we heard a heavy cannonade and it seems Fort Washington was firing on the trenches which he had opened against the fort.

12 November - Today we received orders to be ready to march tomorrow.

13 November - We were ready but did not move out.

16 November - Today the glorious affair was undertaken which earned Lieutenant General von Knyphausen such great honor, that is, the capture of Fort Washington. The Stirn Brigade marched out of camp at seven o'clock. The Donop Regiment remained behind to protect the camp. The attack from this side was supported by some English regiments and our entire force was commanded by Lord Percy. Lieutenant General von Knyphausen led the attack from the other side with the Lossberg, Wutginau, Knyphausen, Rall, and Huyn Regiments. Here the enemy had strong abatis which were nevertheless poorly defended. In four hours they were driven from all these positions and we advanced so near the fort that they could not bring their cannons to bear. Lieutenant General von Knyphausen encountered far more resistance. Nevertheless our troops, under the most severe cannon and small arms fire, overcame the steepest rock formations and abatis. The enemy, on his side also, was forced to withdraw into the fort, whereby General Knyphausen had the advantage for entering the fort, and made preparations for taking it by storm. But first the captain offered them the opportunity to surrender. The occupants requested half an hour to consider the offer, which was granted. As soon as this time expired, they considered it advisable to raise a white flag rather than face an assault, whereupon the entire garrison of 3,800 men stacked arms and surrendered as prisoners of war. Colonel von Loos ordered me to take 45 flankers and we captured 21 prisoners. The loss on our side, including officers, was 351 dead and wounded. About six o'clock our regiment took all the prisoners to Harlem, put them in houses and barns, and guarded them. The number of cannons which the rebels had in the fort amounted to 94. All the regiments returned to their camps except the 10th, which reinforced us at Harlem.

18 November - Today we brought all of the prisoners to the road leading to New York, where we delivered them to the 1st English Brigade, which transported them to New York. Today the Leib, Wutginau, Ditfurth, Prince Charles, Huyn, and Buenau Regiments, as well as two English brigades, encamped near New York, were designated to be shipped to Rhode Island.

21 November - We received the news today that General Cornwallis with the English Guards and the English and Hessian Grenadiers had crossed to New Jersey from near Philipse Manor and captured the rebels' Fort Lee, where twenty 12- and 32-pound cannons, as well as baggage, had been abandoned. His Excellency, the commanding general, renamed Fort Washington, Fort Knyphausen today.

25 November - Today the Rall Regiment moved close to us, into camp on the North River, later to be transferred across to New Jersey.

26 November - Today the quarters' lists were published, a sign that New York will soon be occupied.

29 November - Today the quarters in New York were assigned and we are to move in tomorrow.

30 November - Because nothing was prepared, we still can not move into winter quarters.

Fourth Section

From moving into winter quarters at New York until the opening of the second campaign.

5 December - The Stirn Brigade marched to New York to enter winter quarters, as did the Truembach Regiment, which until now had remained on Staten Island. The Hereditary Prince Regiment and that regiment moved into the barracks. Donop Regiment and our regiment were assigned the houses belonging to rebels. The city lies at the end of a small island with one side exposed to the bay. It is surrounded on both sides by the East and North Rivers. The view toward Jersey is excellent. There are 3,000 or more houses, of which, however, nearly 400 and two churches were laid in ashes on 2 September, and prior to the present rebellion the population was estimated at 18,000 inhabitants. It is about a mile and one-half long and a mile wide. The college on the North River, as well as other public buildings, is very beautiful. The churches are very pretty and include: the Holy Trinity Church, which together with the High German Lutheran Church, burned down, St. Paul's English, the new or St. George's English Chapel, two Dutch Reformed, one German Reformed, one French Reformed, as well as a Quaker Meeting House, one for the Presbyterian, one for the Mennonite Brothers, and a Jewish Synagogue. The barracks can hold 800 to 1,000 men. The city hall and the prisoners' house, called the jail, are very fine buildings. Also Fort George, because of its fortifications, as well as its location, should not be forgotten. This province lies along the 40⁰ north latitude and 75⁰ west longitude from London.

17 December - Today His Excellency, the commanding general-in-chief, arrived here from Jersey to take up winter quarters. We received confirmed reports that Lieutenant Colonel [William] Harcourt of Burgoyne's Regiment of Light

Cavalry had captured the famous General [Charles] Lee outside his lines. A French colonel was captured with him.

20 December - The Truembach Regiment marched out from here to relieve the Koehler Grenadier Battalion at Fort Knyphausen. The latter then came here and on

21 December - embarked on four ships, taking along four 18-pound cannons, and were disembarked at Amboy and marched from there toward Colonel Donop's Brigade. The winter quarters are therefore divided, thus:

New York - English and Hessian headquarters.

English generals: 1) General-in-chief Howe 2) [Samuel] Cleaveland of the Artillery 3) Governor [William] Tryon 4) Commandant [James] Robertson 5) Johnson 6) Quartermaster General Erskine.

Hessian Generals: 1) Lieutenant General von Heister 2) Lieutenant General von Knyphausen 3) Major Generals Stirn 4) Von Mirbach, and 5) Schmidt. The last two are sick.

Regiments: 17th Light Cavalry, the 4th, 15th, 27th, and 45th Infantry, and Stirn's Brigade, consisting of the Hereditary Prince, Donop, and Mirbach Regiments.

In the harbor are six warships, and the admiral commanding all ships in America, [Richard], Lord Howe, has his quarters in the city, also.

Fort Knyphausen - 1) Schmidt's Brigade, consisting of the Truembach, Stein, and Wissenbach Regiments, and 2) The 1st English Brigade.

Kingsbridge - The 4th English Brigade. These three brigades [at Fort Knyphausen and Kingsbridge] are commanded by His Excellency, Lieutenant General von Knyphausen and because the barracks have not yet been completed, the Schmidt Brigade is still camping.

New Jersey - Two English Brigades, Hessian Jaegers, Donop Grenadier Brigade, Rall Brigade, and the Waldeck Regiment, all under General Grant's command.

Rhode Island - Nine English regiments, Lossberg Brigade, consisting of the Leib, Prince Charles, and Ditfurth Regiments, and the Huyn Brigade, consisting of the Wutginau, Huyn, and Buenau Regiments, all of which are commanded by Lord Percy and Lieutenant General [Henry] Clinton.

28 December - We received the sad news that at eight o'clock in the morning of the 26th the Rall Brigade at Trenton in New Jersey was attacked by 13,000 rebels and nearly everyone was made captive. Lieutenant [Jakob] Baum, who with Lieutenant [Johann Nikolaus] Vaupel and Ensign [Ludwig Ferdinand] von Geyso of Knyphausen Regiment escaped, and who arrived here first, confirmed the brigade's misfortune. Captain [Henrich Ludwig] Boecking and Lieutenant [Johannes] Stoebel (of Rall Regiment), Ensign [Henrich Reinhard] Hille (of Lossberg), and Ensign [Henrich Christoph] Zimmermann (of Knyphausen), who were on command, have also escaped. Fortunately, about 500 men got away. All flags and cannons were captured. Colonel [Johann Gottfried] Rall, who commanded, would not accept a parole and, according to reports, has died. Major [Karl Friedrich] von Dechow (of Knyphausen) has died of his wounds, and most of the officers were either killed or wounded.

5 January 1777 - Today a rebel ship richly laden with a great amount of rum and other cargo was brought into the harbor. All the rebels had been sent aboard other ships except for the owner. As he came on land, he pulled a concealed pistol and shot himself.

14 January - The prisoner, General Lee, was brought from Brunswick to the city hall, where the main guard is. One captain, one officer, and twelve men are assigned to his guard every day. No one is allowed to visit him.

17 January - There were reports that the rebels planned to attack Paulus Hook. However, this was a false rumor.

18 January - This morning at eight o'clock the rebels attacked Fort Independence on the other side of Kingsbridge.

However, they were driven back with the loss of one cannon. Today was the Queen's birthday. His Excellence, General Howe, was awarded the Order of the Bath. In turn, he presented a very beautiful fireworks display this evening at seven o'clock. There was also a ball and a grand supper. All the officers were invited. All the reserve pickets were on duty to prevent any disturbances in the streets. The regiment was also under orders to fall out at the first signs of alarm.

19 January - This morning the rebels again attacked Fort Independence, but were again forced to pull back. Captain [Alexander] von Wilmowsky of Truembach Regiment, who was commanding there, earned much honor for his preparedness and good conduct.

20 January - A fire broke out in Prince Street at nine o'clock this evening. One of the murderous arsonists was caught, but the other escaped.

1 February - We learned today that the rebels had pulled back thirty miles from Fort Independence, possibly for the following reason: Six English regiments returned from Rhode Island in order to create a diversion. They dropped anchor near Hell Gate. They may have caused the rebels to believe they would be cut off from their supply depots at Rochelle in Connecticut. Therefore they retired. These six battalions then sailed back a short way and dropped anchor so that at any time they would be ready to strike.

2 February - Today we heard that the rebels had planned to attack two English regiments at Princeton in Jersey. These got reports of the attack and were on the alert. General Erskine led the successful resistance which resulted in the rebels pulling back with the loss of 100 men. The English losses were one officer and thirteen men.

5 February - His excellence, Lieutenant Colonel von Schieck, today assumed command of the Rall Brigade which in the future will be called the Combined Battalion.

7 February - The above mentioned battalion was organized with five companies.

8 February - That battalion was embarked and the destination was Amboy.

16 February - As the commandant, Robertson, has left for England, General [Robert] Pigot has assumed that position [New York city commandant].

25 February - According to Regimental Quartermaster Mueller of the Knyphausen Regiment, who has visited our prisoners of war in New Castle, they are being well-cared for and he also said that after the rebels were victorious at Trenton, their courage has improved and they have received an astonishing number of new recruits.

26 February - The commanding general-in-chief journeyed to Brunswick. He was escorted there from Amboy by five English battalions and a squadron of light dragoons.

9 March - Today he returned from Brunswick to this garrison again, escorted by nine English battalions. Our Colonel von Loos received command of the Lossberg Regiment as recognition of his previous accomplishments and we received Colonel [Justus Henrich] Block in his stead. Lieutenant Colonel [Georg Emanuel] von Lengercke of Prince Charles Regiment received command of the Block Grenadier Battalion. [Thereafter known as the Lengercke Grenadier Battalion.] With this packetboat I received my 2nd lieutenant patent. Captain [Johann Friedrich Zacharias] Wagner of the Huyn Garrison Regiment cut his throat with a razor tonight due to melancholy brought on by a prolonged illness.

19 March - Today three English regiments under the command of Lieutenant Colonel Perth [Lieutenant Colonel John Bird] were embarked on the North River. It is believed they are an expedition to Peekskill.

23 March - His Excellence, Colonel von Schieck, returned to New York from Amboy. His Excellence, Colonel von Loos, has assumed command over the battalion. The first mentioned brought the report that many were deserting from the rebels.

27 March - Today Lieutenant Colonel Perth returned from Peekskill with his detachment. He had destroyed a magazine there. His losses amounted to approximately six officers and forty men.

28 March - The above detachment received a commendation today from the commanding general for its good conduct.

1 April - Today three enemy prize ships were brought in. They were loaded with munitions and each had an estimated value of 12,000 pounds sterling.

5 April - Today the admiral's ship, which previously had remained in the East River, moved, with many other warships and transports, into the North River, and we anticipate an expedition is about to be undertaken.

6 April - Many deserters came in. A ship of the fleet which arrived in the harbor today with provisions from Ireland, sank.

7 and 8 April - Thirty-six heavy cannons and a large amount of ammunition were put aboard ship.

13 April - Today a colonel, six officers, one adjutant general, and 88 privates of the rebel army were brought from Brunswick as prisoners. Our troops had attacked the enemy on the twelfth, not far from Brunswick. About 200 men had been killed and these captured, as well as three metal cannons.

14 April - An enemy privateer, which had been captured in Delaware Bay and had 92 men on board, was brought in here.

15 April - An embarkation list of the entire corps was requested.

20 April - Today Governor Tryon was named commander of the provincial troops.

15 May - Major General Johns was designated as commandant of Fort Knyphausen.

23 May - The Stirn Brigade, as well as the 4th, 15th, 23rd, 27th, 44th, and 64th Regiments, received the order to remain ready for embarkation. At the same time the commanding general ordered that the officers should take nothing with them except that which was absolutely necessary for the campaign. The heavy baggage is to remain in New York.

27 May - Today the order of 23 May was repeated, to be ready on the shortest notice to embark.

31 May - Today the Prince Charles Regiment, which returned from Rhode Island with the Leib Regiment, marched toward Kingsbridge and it was also announced that the Hereditary Prince Regiment, because it is very weak due to illness, would remain in New York and that its place would be taken by the Leib Regiment.

2 June - A fleet of seventeen ships arrived, on board which were 400 Hessian recruits as well as two battalions and one jaeger company from Ansbach.

4 June - Today we received, in addition to the regiments previously mentioned in the embarkation order of 23 may, the order to be standing ready on the common place at six o'clock in the morning in order to be embarked at the King's Wharf on the North River.

Fifth Section

From the opening of the second campaign until the entering of winter quarters.

5 June - Yesterday's orders were carried out this morning when the designated regiments assembled on the common place and thereafter our regiment as sent aboard the assigned ships according to the following:

Jenny - Colonel Block, Captain Rothe, Lieutenants von Toll and Schraidt, Ensign von Drach, and Regimental Surgeon Gechter.

New Blessing - Lieutenant Colonel von Schieck, Captains Reichhold and [Georg] Krug, Lieutenant von Boyneburg, and Ensign Wiessenmueller.

Mermaid - Majors von Biesenrodt and [Hieronymus] Berner, Regimental Quartermaster Schmidt, and me.

Lord Howe - Captain Endemann, Lieutenants Riemann and von Wurmb, Ensign Bulzingsloewen, and Chaplain [Rudolph Reinhard] Virnau.

7 June - We sailed from New York with a wind which was not the best, knowing however, no less than the ship's captain as to our destination.

8 June - We had to tack constantly because the wind was completely contrary.

9 June - This morning the wind was a bit better. At ten o'clock we could see Port Amboy, the capital city of Jersey, situated on a peninsula between the Raritan and Amboy Rivers. At one o'clock we dropped anchor and prepared at once to disembark, which happened. Toward two o'clock we moved beyond this place into camp with the troops which were already there. This city has a pleasant setting and has something more than 100 houses. The barracks have a capacity of 300 to 400 men. New Jersey lies between the 39^0 and 42^0 north latitude and at about 75^0 west longitude. The eastern border is on the Atlantic Ocean, the western on Pennsylvania and Delaware, the southern on Delaware Bay, and the northern border is on the

Hudson River or the province of New York. Prior to the rebellion New Jersey had an estimated 70,000 inhabitants.

11 June - The two Ansbach battalions and their Jaeger Corps arrived, and at the same time, His Excellence, the commander-in-chief.

12 June - The Combined Battalion and the 1st English Brigade marched into camp at Brunswick, on the other side of the Raritan. This camp was again occupied by the Ansbachers. This evening we received orders to march tomorrow.

13 June - At daybreak the march began in the following order: the Dragoons, on foot, Ansbach and English Jaegers, as an advance guard, Queen's Rangers covered the right flank, the mounted Dragoons, Stirn's Brigade, proceeded by two 12-pound cannons, the 4th, 44th, 15th, 17th, 64th, 38th, 27th, 46th, 10th, 23rd, and 40th Regiments. The 55th Regiment, two battalions of Ansbach, and the Waldeck Regiment remained at Amboy. About twelve o'clock we arrived at Brunswick and the Stirn Brigade went into camp on this side of the Raritan.

14 June - I went to Brunswick to see that place. It has about 150 houses and a barracks for 300 men. The city lies in a valley close to the Raritan River.

15 June - At twelve o'clock in the night we received orders to march at two o'clock. This we did at the appointed time. The Koehler Grenadier Battalion, the Combined Battalion, and an English brigade remained on the other side of the Raritan, as well as the baggage which was all left behind, in order to provide a cover force for that place. We marched to the area of Middlebush, an hour to the left of Brunswick and a half hour beyond Milstrom. Here we had an over abundance of groceries. Prior to our march out of the camp at Brunswick our regiment lost Colonel Block due to an illness and Lieutenant Colonel von Schieck assumed command.

16 June - We moved forward a half hour, and here the enemy was met on all sides.

17 and 18 June - We were employed constructing batteries. The headquarters took the name of the area, Middlebush.

19 June - At daybreak everyone returned to Brunswick, having accomplished our objective, and again went into camp on this side of the Raritan. During the march our rear guard was harassed but our side had no casualties.

20 June - It was announced that Major von Biesenrodt was transferred to the Leib Regiment and that Grenadier Captain von Wilmowsky, currently with the Lossberg Regiment, had been promoted to major and transferred to our regiment.

21 June - The Koehler Grenadier Battalion marched toward Amboy in order to escort General [John] Vaughan, who had been assigned to command of the troops at that place.

22 June - The entire army left the region of Brunswick, marching from the right, to Amboy. The Jaegers, covering the right flank, were attacked, but again with no casualties. Stirn Brigade and two English brigades crossed the Raritan to Staten Island and went into camp near Prince's Bay.

24 June - His Excellence, Lieutenant General von Heister, left the army today to return to New York, and it was made known to the army that he was returning to Hesse, and that His Excellence, Lieutenant General von Knyphausen had been given the command. At eight o'clock this morning, completely unexpected, the Stirn Brigade received orders to embark and we entered our previously utilized ships, which were lying at anchor. I had the misfortune of spending the time until five o'clock this afternoon in my boat, because shortly after I left the land, a wind storm arose which caused the sailors to cry for help and only with great effort did we reach the ship. The boat remained tied to the ship while the wind and tide continued.

25 June - At three o'clock this afternoon all the ships, which had the Stirn Brigade on board, were ordered to raise anchor and sail to Amboy. An hour later, Captain [Friedrich Ernst von] Muenchhausen, adjutant to the general-in-chief, came and brought every ship's commander the order to provide the troops with three days' rations. At midnight we debarked and after the Stirn Brigade assembled at Amboy, marched on

26 June - at daybreak, by columns from the right. Our march was to Woodbridge and Westfield, where English headquarters was established and which is about eighteen miles from Amboy, with Brunswick on our right. Meanwhile the Koehler Grenadier Battalion, an English battalion, two Ansbach regiments, and the Waldeck Regiment remained at Amboy. The Combined Battalion, Donop Regiment, and two English regiments commanded by Colonel von Loos occupied the route to Brunswick. The march was very tiring in the extreme heat. The Jaegers and the English Light Infantry were engaged with the enemy from morn until night. The Minnigrode Grenadier Battalion had the good fortune to capture two metal cannons built in France from the enemy, and the English Guards also captured two of the same quality. The battalion suffered seven men wounded, and according to reports made by two deserters, the rebels lost nearly 600 men, 82 of whom we captured. Our regiment lost two non-commissioned officers and two privates who remained behind too long and we assume they were captured.

27 June - At ten-thirty the entire army marched away from the left. The march was very strenuous again and the day unbearably hot, to which was added a shortage of beverages. Our regiment lost a man who was so worn out by the heat and the march that he dropped dead. At dusk we halted and bivouacked during the night. The headquarters and the region are called Basray.

28 June - We continued our march toward Amboy and upon our arrival, our regiment and the Leib Regiment were immediately embarked on the previously utilized ships. Donop Regiment and the Combined Battalion, having left the ships in the morning in order to secure the road to Brunswick, returned and immediately went aboard their ships.

Rueffer Journal

29 June - Part of the army was transferred over to Staten Island.

30 June - The rest of the army, numbering about 8,000 men, followed. Now all of Old and New Jersey has been evacuated. About four o'clock all the ships left the harbor and proceeded to Prince's Bay, where we anchored for the night.

1 July - At daybreak we raised anchor. But because the wind was contrary, after going only a short distance, we again had to drop anchor. About three o'clock the wind improved and by seven o'clock in the evening we lay at King's Ferry on Staten Island, where we dropped anchor.

2 to 4 July - We remained in the same place. The Grenadiers and all the above mentioned troops are still in camp on Staten Island.

5 July - At four o'clock in the afternoon all the ships which had troops on board approached the shore and each day two boat-loads of soldiers were allowed to go walking on the shore. General Clinton is reported to have returned to New York from London today.

6 July - We worked very hard getting the horses and baggage on board.

8 July - Some English regiments and one Ansbach regiment were embarked.

9 July - The Grenadiers and the Combined Battalion and all the English regiments, as well as the Light Cavalry and for the most part, all the rest of the army embarked.

13 July - The order came that tomorrow everyone was to be aboard his ship and we hope to sail soon. The Koehler Grenadier Battalion, four English regiments, both Ansbach battalions, and the Waldeck Regiment were transferred to New York.

14 July - General Stirn came from New York.

15 July - Twelve ships came in today which were in part loaded with Scottish troops and in part with provisions.

16 July - Another ship came in but no one knows which port he came from.

17 July - We again received permission to go to New York, and our hopes of an early departure were for nought, but were again raised because the admiral's ship and other warships came from New York and anchored with our fleet. Therefore no use was made of the permission [to go to New York].

18 July - We received orders upon our debarkation to carry two days' pork, four days' rum, and four days' bread, and at the same time we were ordered to be on our best behavior, because the general had reason to believe [the area] which the army was about to occupy had been forced to take part in the rebellion and the indiscriminate seizure of horses and other livestock was strictly forbidden.

19 July - This afternoon a fleet arrived consisting of five frigates, thirteen ships loaded with hay, and seven small prizes captured from the rebels.

20 July - At ten o'clock this morning the signal to get under sail was given, the anchor was raised at once, and the signal complied with. Our brigade was in the last division, therefore we had to let all the other ships pass. We were just ready to raise the anchor when the wind shifted so that those which had first gotten under way again had to drop anchor. Toward twelve o'clock the wind was a bit better and stronger and a second signal was made to depart. The ships had considerable difficulty in clearing the harbor however. At five o'clock we anchored again near Sandy Hook, in part because the wind had become contrary again, in part because all the warship escorts were not yet arrived. [Words appear to be missing in the German text, but this is the apparent meaning.]

21 July - The ships which had been too far from the fleet came closer and dropped anchor. The ships which had remained in the harbor arrived at our fleet today with a good wind. The warships however remained lying in the harbor. Today we received an order from His Excellence, Lieutenant General von

British/Hessian fleet 23 July 1777 (approx. 300 sail)

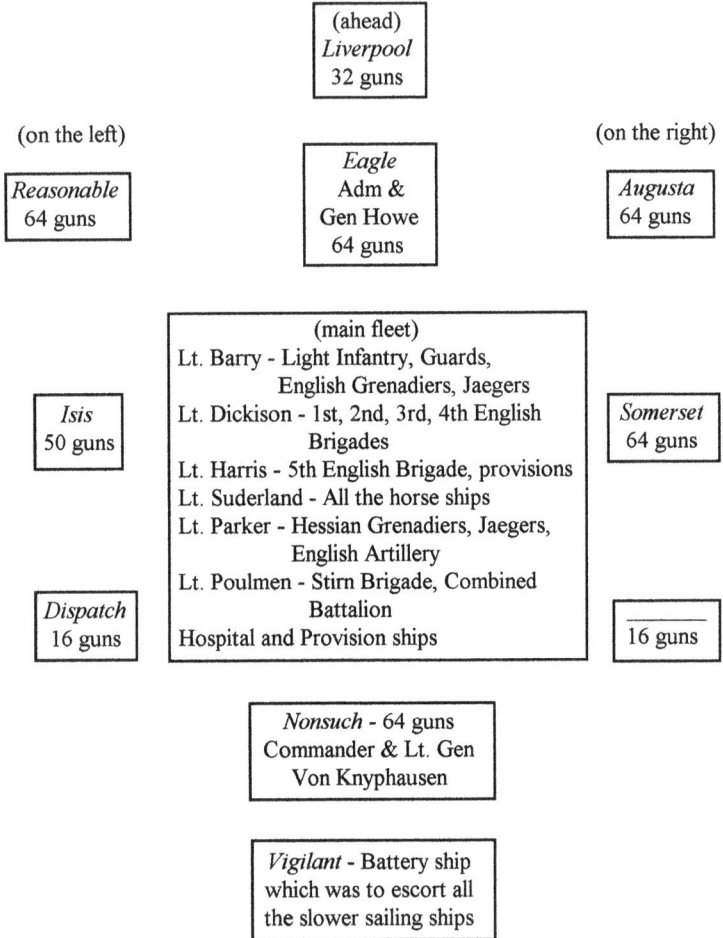

(ahead)
Liverpool
32 guns

(on the left)

Reasonable
64 guns

Eagle
Adm &
Gen Howe
64 guns

(on the right)

Augusta
64 guns

Isis
50 guns

(main fleet)
Lt. Barry - Light Infantry, Guards,
    English Grenadiers, Jaegers
Lt. Dickison - 1st, 2nd, 3rd, 4th English
    Brigades
Lt. Harris - 5th English Brigade, provisions
Lt. Suderland - All the horse ships
Lt. Parker - Hessian Grenadiers, Jaegers,
    English Artillery
Lt. Poulmen - Stirn Brigade, Combined
    Battalion
Hospital and Provision ships

Somerset
64 guns

Dispatch
16 guns

16 guns

Nonsuch - 64 guns
Commander & Lt. Gen
Von Knyphausen

Vigilant - Battery ship
which was to escort all
the slower sailing ships

Knyphausen, that when we debark, the soldiers should take their knapsacks with them and that all should proceed in the best order and in silence.

22 July - We remained at anchor as the wind was contrary and too weak.

23 July - At about eight o'clock in the morning the warships which had remained behind came out to our fleet but stayed under sail and the fleet followed after them with a northeast wind. It was a lovely day. Toward midday the sea became peaceful and the wind blew so gently that we hardly moved. In the afternoon, about four o'clock, the wind improved and we sailed in the following order: [See accompanying chart.]

24 July - Northeast wind and good weather. Our fleet consisted of nearly 300 sail. The view is too pleasant and brilliant to describe. Neither Jersey nor Long Island can any longer be distinguished this morning. Toward three o'clock we could again see Jersey. Our course was south. After a given signal, toward evening, the fleet took another course toward the southeast and we again lost sight of land.

25 July - East by southeast wind and again fine weather. The voyage goes very slowly because the wind is weak. Toward noon we could again see land.

26 July - South by southeast wind and rather strong, at the same time a nice day. This morning we could still see land but because we changed our course toward east-southeast, we soon lost sight of it again. About ten o'clock the wind picked up and during the afternoon developed into a violent storm. At about three o'clock we experienced a dangerous moment. Just as our ship was turning, the *Lord Howe* bore down on our ship under full sail and caused a jarring crash that can not be described. *Lord Howe* broke the cut-water, or the so-called sock mast, completely off. No less damaging, one of our anchors, which had a circumference of eighteen inches and was fastened on the side, broke through and ruined the entire outboard side of our cabin. The *Lord Howe* at the same time suffered even greater damage. Most of his sails were torn and a large part of his cabins were left on our ship, and furthermore, as our sailors say, our anchor did great damage and gouged a great hole in his side. Our sailors inspected our ship as soon as the two ships, with the greatest effort, had been separated, and found to our dismay that we had taken much water and we were thereafter compelled to assign six men daily to pumping every second hour. Each hour the water rose one foot. Because the storm continued to worsen, many people became seasick.

   27 July - Northwest wind but very light. The course is southwest. This night, about twelve o'clock, the storm began to abate and after this time we slept rather peacefully.

   28 July - South-southwest wind and very foggy weather. The course was south-southeast. About noon the wind switched to the north but was not steady. Thunder storms caused the sky to be very dark. Toward evening the ship changed direction and at that time there was a heavy thunder storm and the lightning and thunder claps more violent than we are accustomed to in Germany.

   29 July - East-southeast wind and fine weather. The course is west-southwest. Yesterday's storms had scattered the ships very widely, but gradually they came together again. It was the most peaceful day of our entire trip.

   30 July - West-northwest wind and beautiful bright weather. Our course was northwest. This morning we could see part of Pennsylvania [present Delaware] to our left. It may be Cape James or Cape Henlopen. With a relatively favorable wind we drew steadily nearer and toward midday were close to Delaware Bay, where a lighthouse has been built for the safety of ships. At twelve o'clock we changed direction and separated ourselves from the land, sailed back toward land again toward evening, and lay still off the coast without dropping an anchor.

   31 July - Until ten o'clock this morning we had calm wind. We could still see the land clearly. The wind for entering the bay could not be better and we hope when it becomes a bit stronger that will happen. Toward ten o'clock the wind began to blow well, nevertheless we moved away from the land and at twelve o'clock it was lost from view. About four o'clock we again sailed toward the land. If the wind continues this way we hope to again get close enough to the harbor during the night so that we can enter at daybreak tomorrow. Our joy was spoiled however, as the fleet changed course again at seven o'clock. No one can guess the reason why we have sailed from the land again and continue to cruise while the wind remains so favorable.

1 August - Southwest wind and beautiful weather. We remained all morning on the same course as yesterday and the wind was very favorable for us on this course to the south. This evening we again changed course and sailed toward the land.

2 August - South-southwest wind, beautiful weather, and the same course as yesterday. Toward eight o'clock we changed course and sailed to the southeast and the hope of seeing land soon disappeared again. At one o'clock this midday our hopes were renewed as we again turned toward land, but if we will continue on this course, we will find out this evening or tomorrow morning. If we remain on this course we hope to reach land again tomorrow.

3 August - Southwest wind and continued fine weather. As we are on a new course to the south again this morning our hopes of yesterday have been nullified again. At twelve-thirty this afternoon we again took our old customary course to the southwest.

This day we, and all who are on our ship, hold in memory because as the result of a thunder storm our lives were placed in an incomparably frightful fear of death. Toward six o'clock we saw thunder and lightning in the distance. At this time the admiral gave a signal to change course toward the southeast. Our ship had hardly turned when the storm hit with indescribably frightful thunder and lightning and so suddenly that the crew, because of the terrible storm and hurricane winds which it carried, nearly were robbed of their sense to lower the sails, which resulted in the ship being rolled far over on its left side and nearly covered by waves, so that we were sure that we would be drowned in the inevitable sinking of the ship. The wind, coming from the right side, tore all the upper sails to shreds and then, as the wind slackened after a while, the ship rolled slowly from the left side to the right side and our fear of entering eternity, at this time, generally began to abate. Everyone involved turned his first thoughts to giving thanks to heaven for having saved him from this danger. The storm continued until about ten o'clock but the lightning continued throughout the night. The admiral fired four cannon shots to signal to the fleet that he was stopping and all the warships acknowledged the signal with four cannon shots.

4 August - Southwest wind but so light as to be unnoticeable. It was a bright and very hot day. Toward five o'clock this afternoon the wind improved and the journey went more quickly. According to our present course, it appears we are headed toward Maryland. Our crew reckons us to be 51 miles from Cape Charles in Maryland and 60 miles from the Delaware Bay.

5 August - Southwest wind and fine weather. Our course is no longer that of yesterday, toward Maryland, but southward. This night about twelve o'clock we had another storm but our ship's captain from experience in the last one, had become more careful and lowered the sails soon enough, even though the wind was not as strong at that moment. The storm fortunately passed by. At one o'clock we again changed course. From six to twelve o'clock this night we again had a violent storm, the lightning indescribably strong, but on the other hand, there were fewer thunder claps. From the first sign the captain lowered all sails as he expected very strong winds. Such winds came and with such force and darkness that the captain let us hang a lantern in the cabin. The movement of the ship was bearable and we would have born it better than in the last thunder storm, if we had not lowered all the sails.

6 August - South-southwest wind and rainy weather. We frequently changed course although there was more of a calm than wind. Toward evening we again had a storm, which however, was not very strong and passed to one side. Nothing but the dreadful weather made us wish to reach land soon, as the more we neared the southern regions, the more often and stronger, we had to expect such.

7 August - Still calm and a bright day. Toward noon a south-southwest wind and rather strong so that we could sail some miles in an hour. At twelve-thirty we could see land on the left side but did not know its name. The crew was not pleased with this as they could see that we had been driven too far to the north.

8 August - West-southwest wind and a clear, warm day. Since seven o'clock this morning we have again been on our southerly course, and hope, if we continue, by the end of this week to change the misery of life aboard ship for life on land.

9 August - Still the same wind, and with fine weather, rather strong. At sundown we changed course again. Until 12 August, southwest wind and nothing new.

12 August - South-southwest wind and fine weather. We find less depth than yesterday and with every casting of the lead the water becomes more shallow. We are still on the same old course. Toward six o'clock in the evening, completely unhoped-for and still quite far away, we saw Cape Charles. Hardly had we seen this than the admiral signaled a change of course, and as it was nearly night, we soon lost sight of the land once again. This morning was one year since we first saw land in America after our long sea voyage from England.

13 August - West-southwest wind and not as good as yesterday. The old course.

14 August - West-southwest wind, fine weather but calm. Toward two o'clock in the afternoon the wind became so good that toward five o'clock we could once again see Cape Charles.

Tomorrow we hope perhaps to reach our destination, if the wind will remain so good.

15 August - South-southwest wind and a day hotter than customary in Germany. This night toward eleven o'clock the admiral gave the signal to anchor with three cannon shots and two lanterns on the middlemast and our ship's captain complied at twelve o'clock. Cape Charles can be seen clearly and we raised anchor and sailed at daybreak. Toward seven o'clock, due to a change in course, we approached Cape Henry, but as it became calm toward midday, we had to anchor. Toward twelve o'clock the wind arose again. However, as we would have had to pass the dangerous sandbanks between Cape Charles and Cape Henry at dusk, a signal ordered us once again to anchor, which was done immediately.

16 August - West-southwest wind and still very warm. At daybreak the anchor was raised but because the winds were too weak and contrary we anchored again at nine-thirty. Toward one o'clock the wind swung to the south and became very favorable and continued so strong that we could travel four to five miles in an hour. And therefore we were so fortunate as to reach Chesapeake Bay and put Cape Henry far behind us. Toward four o'clock a very strong storm arose again and because of the extreme narrows, Virginia on our left and Maryland on our right, it became too dangerous to travel. We therefore dropped anchor at seven o'clock in the evening.

17 August - The storm persisted all night with the strongest lightning and wind. At daybreak we raised the anchor and sailed with the most favorable south wind that we had yesterday. This did not last long however, and because of the developing calm, it became necessary to anchor at ten o'clock. Toward evening a very strong storm arose again, which, for the most part, passed over and we received nothing from it except strong lightning. We lay still all day at anchor because there was absolutely no wind.

18 August - West wind, very favorable and also quite strong. We could travel over four miles an hour. Toward noon it became weaker and then contrary so that we tacked several times, and as it was with little profit, anchored at four o'clock. Nevertheless we had a strong storm, which fortunately however, passed by.

19 August - North-northwest wind and still contrary. Nevertheless at daybreak we raised the anchor, but had to tack. Toward ten o'clock the wind shifted and came from the northeast. At twelve o'clock we had a strong storm with continuous heavy rainfall. The wind improved and we could sail four miles in an hour. At dusk, as usual, we again dropped anchor.

20 August - Northwest wind and rather strong. At six o'clock the anchor was raised. Since yesterday we no longer have Virginia to our left, but Maryland on both sides. At ten o'clock it became calm again. The wind however came again at three o'clock with a violent storm. Toward six o'clock we dropped anchor.

21 August - Southwest wind, very favorable and with fine weather, but because we could not use all the sails in the narrow passage, we covered very little distance. At nine o'clock this morning on our left we saw the capital of Maryland, named Mundeltown or Annapolis, numbering about 160 houses. It lies close to the Chesapeake Bay on a peninsula of land on the Severn River. This and two small streams form the peninsula. Two flags, which were to be seen just outside the city, showed the commander-in-chief's warning of 18 July did not apply, but that the city's inhabitants, like most Americans, were rebels. Through the telescope it could be seen that there were thirteen red and white stripes in these flags, which represented the thirteen provinces. Until about four o'clock we sailed with the most favorable wind, but at this time, exactly as anticipated, we dropped anchor at Swan Point. At six o'clock a signal called all the ships' captains to their agent in order to receive instructions.

Our ship's quartermaster (the captain was sick) brought the news that as soon as we anchored tomorrow, the flatboats from the ships should be brought around, also that we were about twenty miles from Baltimore, where we had expected to debark. The reason we had so unexpectedly anchored was because the admiral thought the rebels had closed the river with sunken obstacles. Therefore in order to check this out, he had sent several small, armed ships ahead. There still has not been a day since we arrived in this warm region when we have not experienced a storm, except today.

22 August - Still the good wind of yesterday. Toward five o'clock we raised the anchor, but because the wind was very weak, we did not sail very far . At eleven o'clock we anchored again and in Elk River. The flatboats, in compliance with yesterday's order, were immediately ordered into the water. We had to go through a narrow passage which small ships had marked by putting out white flags. Toward five-thirty a boat carrying a sea officer notified the fleet to anchor as close as possible between the admiral and the battery ship *Vigilant*. Therefore this was done at six o'clock. On our entire voyage we have not been as close to land as we are now. We again had a violent storm, but without serious consequences.

23 August - Continued good winds. At eight o'clock we raised the anchor and it appeared that we had still not reached our destination. However, we had only traveled two or three miles when we again anchored. At one o'clock a cannon shot with a designated flag called all regimental commanders to the admiral's ship *Eagle*. Today we had a stronger storm than any heretofore.

24 August - We lay quietly at anchor. On a given order all the flatboats were called to the admiral's ship and there is no longer any doubt that this is the place where we shall once again stand on solid ground. At eight o'clock this morning a signal from the admiral's ship re-affirmed the 18 July order to go on land with provisions, and these were immediately issued. We hope to debark this afternoon. Toward two o'clock this afternoon His Excellence, Lieutenant General von Knyphausen, had himself transferred aboard the *Elizabeth* because the *Nonsuch*, due to shallow water, could no longer sail farther.

25 August - This morning we raised the anchor and sailed a few miles farther on Elk River and anchored at two o'clock. From that place we could see, only a short distance away, that the English and Hessian Grenadiers had already landed. Toward evening our brigade also began to land. Major Wilmowsky with fifty men was also fortunate enough to land by Elk's Ferry. But as evening came on too quickly and the admiral was traveling around in the fleet, and further, as a strong storm struck, the admiral ordered that no further landings be made this evening. And we therefore had to spend another night aboard ship. According to the orders issued, the debarkation was made in the following order:

I Debarkation - Under General Earl Cornwallis, and under him, Colonel von Donop. The 1st and 2nd Battalions of Light Infantry, the 1st and 2nd Battalions of Grenadiers, and the Hessian and Ansbach Jaegers.

II Debarkation - Hessian Grenadiers, Queen's Rangers, Guards, 4th and 23rd Regiments.

III Debarkation - 38th [or possibly 28th], 49th, 5th, 10th, 27th, 40th, 55th, 15th, and 42nd Regiments.

IV Debarkation - 44th, 17th, 33rd, 37th, 46th, 64th, and 71st Regiments.

V Debarkation - Stirn Brigade, consisting of the Leib, Donop, and Mirbach Regiments, and the Combined Battalion.

26 August - This morning at daybreak the flatboats for our debarkation arrived and we went on land at Elk's Ferry. We stood around in confusion, without tents because they had been left aboard ship. This region is called Turkey Point and belongs to Maryland. The Light Infantry and Grenadiers under the command of General Howe marched six miles farther, to the Head of Elk, or Elktown, where they captured, in the river with this name, several ships with useful supplies, among others, a great amount of tobacco. The troops under General Howe were the following: Hessian and Ansbach Jaegers, 1st and 2nd Battalion of Light Infantry, Queen's Rangers, English Jaegers, English Grenadiers, 1st Artillery Brigade, Hessian Grenadiers, 2nd Artillery Brigade, English Guards, 1st and 2nd English Brigades, 3rd Company of the 16th Dragoon Regiment, and the dismounted Dragoons, and 3rd Battalion of Mountain Scots of the 71st Regiment. The remaining troops, commanded by Lieutenant General von Knyphausen, were: the 3rd Artillery Brigade, Stirn Brigade, 37th, 64th, 46th, and 33rd Regiments.

27 August - Today we received our tents and baggage. We received orders to move to another camp tomorrow.

28 August - This morning at eight o'clock we marched one-half hour farther and set up a regular camp.

29 August - So far we have neither seen nor heard anything of the enemy, although it is reported that the enemy is not far from us. In this stretch of land we have not seen any females because they were told by the rebels that the Hessians would have misused them in an unpleasant manner, so they have all fled.

30 August - Provisions are so rare that one has to be satisfied with nothing but ship's rations. At noon today we received orders to march tomorrow and those among the sick needing special care were sent aboard the hospital ship.

31 August - This morning at six o'clock we resumed our march. At Elk Ferry we embarked and then again debarked on the other side of the river at Cecil Courthouse. All the baggage except the tents was left aboard ship and we hope to get it back again within a few days. As soon as we had reassembled after our debarkation, we marched away in the following order:

The advance guard consisted of the English pickets. Then Lieutenant Wilson followed with a 3-pound cannon. Then the 33rd, 46th, and 37th Regiments. These were followed by the Stirn Brigade, the English and Hessian baggage, and finally the rear guard which consisted of the Hessian pickets. At every house we passed a pardon letter was nailed, and a watch was posted to prevent looting. The headquarters is called Cecil George.

1 September - Today we remained peacefully standing and spent our time collecting all sorts of livestock.

2 September - This morning at four-thirty we struck our tents and at five o'clock marched from the right with full companies, in the following order:

English pickets as an advance guard with two 3-pound cannons. Mounted Dragoons, 1st Battalion of the 71st Regiment, 3rd and 4th Brigades, Stirn Brigade, and the Hessian pickets as a rear guard. The march was about six miles. At twelve o'clock we entered Pennsylvania for the first time and set up camp at Bohema. The headquarters was close to our front and was called Garrison Tavern. During the previous night a detachment of several hundred enemy dragoons spent the night in the camp which we occupy today.

3 September - At six o'clock in the morning, with half companies, we again marched from the right in the same order as yesterday, with the exception that the Hessian pickets patrolled on the sides and half of the Combined Battalion served as the rear guard. The other half, under the command of Colonel von Borck, had to occupy a defile. Toward twelve o'clock we congregated at Aiken's Tavern where the headquarters for Howe's Corps was established. Today for the first time the Jaegers and Light Infantry were sharply engaged with the enemy. Our losses were about twenty men. The loss on the other side is still unknown.

4 September - This afternoon at four o'clock the order suddenly came that all baggage, as well as tents, was to be taken aboard ship. The officers' baggage consisted of nothing but what was on the body.

5 September - Today the Jaegers, commanded by Lieutenant Colonel [Ludwig Johann August] von Wurmb, received a commendation for their conduct yesterday. According to the statement of a dragoon deserter, the enemy has withdrawn across the so-called Christiana Bridge, which they reportedly had strongly occupied, and their corps, which was commanded by two generals, [Charles] Armand [Tuffin, Marquis de la Rouerie] and [Lieutenant Colonel Louis Casimir de] Holzendorf, of the French service, on the third lost 300 men including those carried as missing.

7 September - At twelve o'clock this day we received orders to be prepared to march within one hour, marching from the left in three divisions.

8 September - According to yesterday's orders this morning at six o'clock the entire army marched from the left in three divisions.

I Division - Under the orders of Lieutenant General [Charles] Earl Cornwallis, 1st and 2nd Battalions of Light Infantry, with one officer and twelve men of the mounted Jaegers, 1st and 2nd Battalions of English Grenadiers, Hessian Grenadiers, Hessian dismounted Jaegers, 1st and 2nd Battalions of English Guards, and the mounted Jaegers.

II Division - Under orders of General Grant, two squadrons of the Queen's Dragoons, 1st Brigade of Artillery, 1st and 2nd English Brigades, 3rd Brigade of Artillery, 3rd and 4th English Brigades, and then the baggage. The 3rd Battalion of the 71st Regiment provided a patrol on the right of the baggage, behind which the livestock followed.

III Division - Under command of Lieutenant General von Knyphausen, Hessian dismounted Jaegers, 2nd Brigade of Artillery, Stirn Brigade, 1st and 2nd Battalions of the 71st Regiment, Queen's Rangers, and English Jaegers. At two o'clock we passed Newark, a very pleasantly built city of about sixty houses, but completely uninhabited. Also, now and again, very pleasing country homes which previous to this time we had seldom encountered in this area because it is rather thinly settled. At eleven o'clock we marched into camp. The headquarters is named after the region, which is called Nowgard. During our march General Cornwallis reportedly bumped into General [William Alexander, Lord] Stirling with about 1,000 men, completely unexpectedly, and because he fled, some wagons with baggage were captured.

9 September - Enemy patrols which were seen at various times today clearly show that the enemy is at no great distance from us. From our camp, the Delaware can be seen at a distance of three miles. At one-thirty the entire army marched in two divisions, with half companies, from the right. The division of General Howe marched on our right. From this date we encountered many owners of houses, most of whom were Quakers and who appeared to be loyal to the crown. Toward evening we crossed a body of water through which we had to wade because there was no bridge. Toward ten o'clock this night our patrols to the sides fired several times and we believed they had encountered parties of the enemy. However it was an adjutant, [Captain Alexander Campbell], from the commander-in-chief with an escort of dragoons bringing an order for General von Knyphausen to change his march because information concerning a change in the enemy's dispositions had been received during the march. Unfortunately the adjutant was fatally wounded. At twelve o'clock this night we marched into camp at King's Square, where the headquarters was set up. This community, which is very pleasantly built, belongs to Fusty County.

10 September - At twelve o'clock we changed our camp and moved forward another half hour, where once again we joined the corps of General Howe. According to statements of two spies who encountered a picket, a forward detachment of the enemy consisting of about 1,000 men, mostly cavalry, is only a quarter-hour away from us and the army is on Brandywine Hill three or four miles from here - a half-hour beyond Kings Square.

11 September - This day has earned the right to special recognition because it has given us the greatest glory. At daybreak the whole army marched in two divisions, by half companies, from the right. General Cornwallis' division, which the commanding general was with, was on our left. General von Knyphausen's division consisting of the following troops assembled on the road to Welsh Tavern: one officer and fifteen dragoons, the English Jaegers, the 1st and 2nd English Brigades, Stirn Brigade, the remaining Dragoons, the 2nd Artillery Brigade, baggage and livestock, and then the rear guard consisting of three battalions of the 71st Regiment, of which the 2nd Battalion covered the rear of the baggage, the 3rd Battalion was on the right flank, and the 1st Battalion was on the left flank. Hardly one and one-half miles had been marched when the most advanced regiments were in a sharp engagement with the enemy, in which they suffered a great loss. Toward nine o'clock, after the most advanced troops captured one height after the another with great difficulty and heavy losses, we received orders not to advance farther and we lay on the heights at Chadds Ford opposite Brandywine Hill, which according to statements by deserters and prisoners was occupied by 24,000 men, who except for a continuous cannonade remained unengaged. Also, the Queen's Rangers and English Jaegers were in continuous hand to hand combat with the most advanced enemy parties. At four o'clock in the afternoon we heard, on our left wing, the heavy fire by Cornwallis' corps, at which instant we moved out and advanced on he enemy's left wing, by Brauntown, or Schatzes Ferry, through the Brandywine Hills and seized them, whereupon the enemy retired in great fear, and in a battery from which he had done us great harm, and which the 4th English Regiment had stormed, he left a Hessian cannon which had been captured at Trenton, two French cannons, and a howitzer. The approaching dusk prevented our pursuit of the enemy. Therefore we camped on the Brandywine Hills. The enemy losses are still not known, but certainly so many that their army has scattered during their flight and is near complete collapse. The bravery displayed by all the English troops today, those under the command of General Cornwallis as well as General von Knyphausen, can not be described with too much enthusiasm. Our loss is still not known. Everyone thinks however that it is very large. The corps commanded by General Cornwallis was also very fortunate having captured a Hessian cannon lost at Trenton, eleven French cannons, and one howitzer. Stirn Brigade lost seven men, of whom two of those killed and one wounded man were from our regiment. The Congress had eaten at a house which we passed today, Welsh's Tavern, and they had strongly recommended that their troops hold Brandywine Hill.

12 September - We remained quiet. The enemy have for the most part withdrawn. [The previous sentence seems to have words missing in the manuscript, but this seems to be the meaning.] Today the commander-in-chief sent his commendation for the good conduct of the troops in yesterday's affair. The English headquarters was at Dalworth, the Hessian's at Brauntown, and the field hospital set up at Talbot.

13 September - We remained in the same camp as yesterday. Our losses consist of 58 English and four German officers killed or wounded, including Captain [Johann Friedrich] Trautvetter from the Hessian and Lieutenant [Karl] von Forstner of the Ansbach Jaegers, Lieutenant von Baumbach of the Guards, and Lieutenant [Konrad] DuPuy of the Linsing Grenadier Battalion, as well as thirty jaegers of the total loss of 400 men, and on the enemy side, about 800 men. According to statements made by deserters, General Washington is at Darby, four miles from Philadelphia. Rumor has it that our fleet has already entered the mouth of the Delaware River and that the 40-gun ship *Roebuck* has sailed up to Wilmington, where our large hospital will soon be established. General Cornwallis marched to Chester today with a part of his corps.

14 September - We remained quiet and are occupied with the search for wounded. The Combined Battalion marched toward Wilmington today, escorting a part of the prisoners and the wounded.

15 September - We learned today that General Washington has withdrawn to Germantown, which provides him with a more advantageous position, also that many transport and provisions ships have already arrived at Wilmington, from which we hope soon to receive beverages and rations as they are very rare here at the present time. At six o'clock this evening we received orders to march tomorrow. Unfortunately our regiment's destination, based on a report from Colonel Loos, is to march to Wilmington, as he feels his force is too weak to combat the rebels there, who are commanded by Generals Rotley [Caesar Rodney ?] and [William] Smallwood.

16 September - At five o'clock this morning the entire army marched from the right. Our regiment crossed the Brandywine Creek, through which we had to wade on the day of the battle at Brandywine Hill, at one o'clock on a bridge near the village of Brandywine. At this village of only about thirty houses, which is separated from Wilmington by this river, we joined the Combined Battalion and two battalions of the 71st Regiment of Scots. This settlement (Wilmington) lies in a pleasant region, contains 120 for the most part, well-constructed houses, and is situated on the side of the Delaware which presents a very pleasant view of the Christiana River and is primarily settled by Quakers, who are mostly still present. The prisoners, except for the wounded, who were initially held at the so-called Gymnasium, number about 325 men. The place was previously known for the fine flour which was produced by its mills. The 44-gun ship *Roebuck*, as well as some smaller ships, sailed farther up the Delaware River today. The fleet is still reported to be some twenty miles from here.

17 September - Our regiment changed camp and moved from the road leading to the Christiana Bridge to the right wing, resting on the road to Philadelphia, which is some 27 miles from here.

18 September - What is now happening to the main army is unknown to us. News reports are very rare. Colonel von Loos was informed by letter yesterday from the commander-in-chief that the commander planned to attack General Wemmes. [possibly Anthony Wayne], day before yesterday, but that he retreated so quickly that he could not be overtaken. We also learned that the army is just half way between Philadelphia and Lancaster, being thirty miles from each place.

19 September - From a captured letter written by an outwardly loyalist-inclined Quaker to a friend in the rebel army, the Quaker expressed his desire to be with his friend in order to avoid the Hessian tyranny. Although the best order and conduct are maintained here, many who secretly support the rebels live here. The author at the moment sits with his comrades at the Gymnasium.

20 September - News from a resident of Philadelphia is to the effect that the enemy army, as well as most of the inhabitants, has fled the city. As the prisoners and wounded are to be put aboard ship as soon as the fleet arrives here, we hope to leave this place soon and to return to the army.

21 September - We are working diligently to fortify our front as well as both flanks. Up to this time the enemy has not disturbed us.

22 September - We have not previously passed through an area where the food was as cheap as here.

23 September - An enemy deserter brought the news today that an enemy corps had been attacked by General Erskine and had suffered 200 dead and wounded.

25 September - This morning about nine o'clock, quite unexpectedly, we heard a heavy cannonade from ships' cannons on the Delaware, mixed with small arms fire. The rebels who still occupied New Jersey with a part of their army had engaged our fleet, which consisted of about eight armed vessels, with a strong battery. Therefore ten flatboats with marines were sent to demolish it. We could clearly see how they landed during the bombardment and disregarding the small arms fire of the enemy, not only carried out their orders but pursued the enemy several miles.

26 September - The news of our army becomes more uncertain each day, and less frequent. Colonel von Loos has learned from an inhabitant from Philadelphia that General Washington had still strongly occupied the bank of the Schuylkill River, because General Howe made him believe he would cross very near the enemy's front, from that place where he then stood. Therefore General Washington had lined the complete bank with artillery. However, General Howe, during the night, had marched twelve miles farther up the river, crossed with the greatest expedition, and stood more nearly in the enemy's rear than in his front.

27 September - The news of yesterday was confirmed. This entire morning we heard a nearly uninterrupted cannonade, whose cause however, is not yet known.

28 September - Through a detachment which came in during the night to Colonel von Loos, the news of the twentieth, that all the inhabitants of Philadelphia had fled, was contradicted. The cannonade of yesterday had been fired by inhabitants of Philadelphia, which had been captured yesterday noon, when General Cornwallis entered the city at eleven o'clock with some English and two battalions of Hessian Grenadiers. The only resistance which he found was a 36-gun frigate by the name of *Delaware* and two gondolas of eight and ten cannons, which fired continuously. As soon as Earl Cornwallis neared the city, a battery of heavy cannons opened fire and sank a gondola, at which the frigate, whose wing was being covered, ran fast aground on a sandbank and so fell into our hands and was also immediately occupied by the King's troops. At the same time Captain Hammond of the *Roebuck* reportedly received the news that the frigate could be refloated by the flood tide and that as soon as the wind and the removal of the *chevaux de frise* would permit him to advance farther up the Delaware River, he was to signal his intended execution of this movement with a cannon shot. Then the rebel fleet, which was lying between Chester and Philadelphia and consisted of ten to twelve frigates and other armed vessels, could be attacked from both sides. Today this news appeared even more so to be founded on fact because at daybreak the fleet, consisting of five frigates which lay here at Wilmington, followed the ship *Roebuck* and sailed up the Delaware. If the ships are so fortunate as to clear out the obstacles, we hope soon to be able to hear the attack. A patrol was sent out today which went as far as Newtown, brought back the news that 800 or 900 rebels reportedly have passed Christiana Bridge six miles from here.

30 September - Colonel von Loos received an order from General Cornwallis at Philadelphia, dated one o'clock on this night, to send a detachment of 200 Scots toward Chester in order not only to maintain communications between Philadelphia and here, but also to provide batteries on land to support the clearing of the *chevaux de frise*, to which purpose this detachment was sent out this morning.

31 September [sic] - At dusk we heard a heavy cannonade mixed with small arms fire. The Scottish Colonel MacDonald, [probably Major Alexander M'Donald] sent a detachment toward Chester to learn the cause.

1 October - We learned from two people who arrived here from Philadelphia that yesterday's firing had been from our frigates against a battery in New Jersey called Billingsport. During this cannonade some English regiments, as well as the Scottish detachment sent from here, had crossed over to destroy it. General Washington should make a movement, according to the reports of these men, to take his army into Jersey and to this end he moves ever nearer the Delaware. General Howe reportedly is near him and actually is at Germantown. An English grenadier who had been made a prisoner of war came in today as a deserter and brought the news that as soon as General Howe turns more toward the south, all the prisoners are to be sent to South Carolina. We learned from the detachment sent out yesterday that those men reported that our row galleys had passed the first row of obstacles in the river, of which the rebels had made three, without accident. During the crossing of the troops to Billingsport, the rebels had planned to send two fire ships against our fleet with the ebb tide, and had set them on fire. However, as the tide turned just at that time, instead of sailing into our fleet, they entered their own fleet and nearly destroyed it.

2 October - Reportedly the enemy militia have withdrawn from Christiana Bridge and only small detachments have been posted along the road to prevent our side from bringing in foodstuffs.

3 October - A message sent from General Cornwallis to Colonel MacDonald gives us hope of moving away from here soon. And it reports that as soon as our fleet arrives here, the hospital and prisoners will be sent aboard ship and we will be rejoined to the army.

4 October - Many residents from this place, who have traveled inland fifteen or twenty miles, have brought dependable information. There are 8,000 to 10,000 rebel militia about ten miles from here, who are on the march from Lancaster to attack us. As a precaution all our pickets have been extended outward and all planks on the Brandywine Bridge have been loosened so that they can be taken up at first alarm. Toward evening we could already see large groups and complete regiments working steadily on defensive positions on the heights which are across from our camp. The approach of darkness prevented more exact observations.

5 October - As sure as I felt that my outposts would be visited by the enemy during the night, nevertheless, we were undisturbed. Above all, all the reports appear to have been false, as a patrol made by Major von Stein encountered absolutely nothing, and no one. [What happened to the large groups seen yesterday?] At noon today a rumor, which is certainly our wish, was spread by a man from Philadelphia, that the main rebel army of 4,000 men, under the command of General Washington, attacked General Howe at Germantown yesterday morning. The rebels won an initial advantage, not only driving our outposts back, but forcing the army, while still not daylight, to retreat and taking many cannons from the English Light Infantry. However, a colonel of the light infantry seized a house in Germantown with his people and prevented the enemy from advancing farther over the bridge at Germantown, on which he could fire from this house, so that General Howe gained the time necessary to regroup and thereby seize the advantage, not only to counter-attack and to retake the captured cannons, but to pursue the enemy for eight miles. The Queen's Rangers and all light troops reportedly have suffered a great deal and it is even said that the Queen's Rangers who survived Brandywine Hill have been completely destroyed. More exact news concerning the losses to both sides is still not available. General Egin [James Agnew ?] is reported killed and General Stirn slightly wounded in the arm.

6 October - The news received yesterday has been confirmed; also, our ships have been fortunate enough to clear the second *chevaux de frise* and we now assume that the attack by both fleets will soon occur, to which a naval officer was sent today to Admiral Howe with the order to send four more armed ships to Chester. These appeared this afternoon at four o'clock on a good wind and as far as we know, they are three frigates and the admiral himself.

8 October - Admiral Howe has sent a flag of truce to Mud Island, lying in the Delaware between Philadelphia and Chester, which the enemy has occupied with a strong force and considers unconquerable. He proposed that if those batteries, which have been supplied with thirteen months provisions and are said to have forty cannons, would surrender, the troops would be allowed to withdraw without opposition. Otherwise they face certain capture as only a few *chevaux de frise* remain in place and Philadelphia is in our hands. The commander reportedly sent back the answer however, that it would not happen until the guns had cooled their freedom's blood. This evening the detachment of Scots arrived here from Chester, but only after they had one man killed, one wounded, and one captured.

9 October - From just before midnight until nine o'clock this morning we have heard a continuous cannon fire and we assume it is either from or against Mud Island.

10 October - A large recruit transport of English and Hessians has reportedly arrived at New York.

11 October - Today we heard a cannonade as strong as the one on 9 October, but do not know the cause and can only assume that our fleet is engaged with the batteries on Mud Island.

12 October - Yesterday evening a portion of the fleet which until now has lain at New Castle arrived at Wilmington. All those who became sick during our voyage from New York and since our last landing, and whose health has improved, were debarked here. The English formed one battalion. The Hessians however, were assigned to the Combined Battalion and to our regiment. All prisoners except those in hospital have been sent aboard ship and according to reports, are to be sent to New York. The fleet is said to have encountered a violent storm as it entered the ocean from Chesapeake Bay, which caused the *Father and Goodwell* to go aground, but the crew were rescued. Also, other ships were reported to have suffered heavy damage. Lieutenant [Friedrich Adam Julius] von Wangenheim of the Jaeger Corps, who was among the convalescents, has been assigned to our regiment. He told us that there were two jaeger companies with the troops which arrived at New York. We also learned that the rebels had made simultaneous attacks on Kingsbridge and Long and Staten Islands, but were driven back at all three places with losses and that at the two latter places the provincial troops have conducted themselves very well, as usual.

14 October - The rebels are reported to be only thirteen miles from here, with the intent of paying us a visit. However, as the embarkation lists have been published with orders to march tomorrow, it follows that we do not need to concern ourselves with them.

15 October - This morning at six o'clock our march began, in the following order:

The Jaegers commanded by Lieutenant von Wangenheim, the English convalescents commanded by Major N. Larat, [or Lamont], the Scottish Brigade, Mirbach Regiment, and the Combined Battalion. We marched from the left. The Jaegers, watches, pickets, and separate detachments were the rear guard. Because of the need to load equipment and horses, we halted in the town and embarkation was begun just at dusk in a rather disorderly fashion. We did not go aboard our assigned ship this evening, but to comply with the order of vacating the town and the region, spent the night aboard small horse sloops where we also met Lieutenant [Johann F. W.] Briede of the Knyphausen Regiment and his men. We still do not know our destination but expect to learn what it is at Chester.

16 October - At seven-thirty this morning the flatboats came to take us to the previously assigned ships. Our regiment was divided as follows:

On *Hundert* - Colonel von Schieck, Lieutenants Schotten, Riemann, and von Toll, and Ensign Bulzingsloewen.

On *Bristol* - Major von Wilmowsky, Captain von Bogatzky, Lieutenant von Boyneburg, Ensign Berner, and me.

On *Mermaid* - Captain Endemann, Lieutenant von Wurmb, Ensign Wiessenmueller, Regimental Surgeon Gechter, and Chaplain Virnau.

And on *Lord Howe* - Captains Reichhold and Rothe, Ensign von Drach, Regimental Quartermaster Schmidt, and Captain Krug of the Artillery.

At ten o'clock we raised anchor and sailed with a contrary wind from the northwest and the flood tide, as most ships do, to Chester, but as soon as the flood had passed, again dropped anchor. At twelve o'clock, in the vicinity of Chester, a heavy cannon fire could be heard. Some thought we were bound for New Jersey.

17 October - Northeast wind, still contrary, and rather stormy. At eight o'clock we raised anchor and sought to reach the fleet at Chester by tacking. Almost at once we sailed too near the land and although in no danger, grounded on the sand, from which we were soon able to work loose by towing with a flatboat, and we sailed on. Toward two o'clock we dropped anchor at Chester and the ship's captain received orders to provide us with two days' rations.

18 October - At daybreak we were landed, marched at ten o'clock, and arrived that evening in camp at King's Town, close to the Schuylkill. About four o'clock we passed the small city of Darby. Philadelphia is another three and one-half miles from here.

19 October - This morning about four o'clock our outposts were alarmed, however without bad results. The enemy army is supposedly in part on this side, and in part on the other side of the Schuylkill and their outposts are only six miles from here. Nevertheless, dependable reports have come in that General Howe has moved with the army from Germantown to the region of Philadelphia. Today a pontoon bridge was built at the ferry across the Schuylkill.

20 October - This morning at three o'clock the two Scottish regiments marched to Darby as an escort for the provisions wagons. General von Knyphausen and Earl Cornwallis were here today to look over our dispositions. At eleven o'clock our pickets were attacked again and two men wounded. We heard a heavy cannonade throughout the day today in the neighborhood of our fleet, Mud Island, and Redbank, which is a fort in New Jersey. At four o'clock the two Scottish regiments returned again. Today, through orders, the army was informed that General Clinton had captured the rebel forts Montgomery, Constitution, Clinton, and Independence, in Connecticut, and thereby opened communications on the Hudson River.

21 October - Late yesterday we received orders to march and at two o'clock this morning our regiment marched over the Schuylkill and at Philadelphia joined with the Linsing, Lengercke, and Minnigerode Grenadier Battalions, and two companies of Jaegers, and under the command of Colonel von Donop, were transferred across the Delaware in flatboats to New Jersey at daybreak. Here we learned for the first time that our destination was to capture Fort Red Bank. As soon as everyone had crossed, we marched and arrived late this evening at Haddonfield, a very pleasant little city of 150 houses, where we camped. Our advance and rear guards were engaged several times with some running troops of the enemy, which resulted in two jaegers being wounded.

22 October - This morning at four o'clock we broke camp and marched on Fort Red Bank, which for most of the corps under the command of Colonel Donop, will certainly remain in our thoughts forever. Toward eleven o'clock we arrived in the neighborhood of the fort. One hundred fascines were made at once by each regiment. After Colonel von Donop appraised the situation at three-thirty in the afternoon, he permitted the fort, through Major [Charles] Stuart and his adjutant, Captain [Johann Emanuel] Wagner, the opportunity of surrender. While this transpired, a detachment of one captain, two officers, and 100 men were commanded to take a position in front of the regiment and to carry the fascines, and the Battalion von Minnigerode on the right, Linsing on the left, and our regiment in the middle, were set in a line ready to storm the fort. The Grenadier Battalion Lengercke and the Jaegers covered our rear. Therefore, when Major Stuart brought back a spiteful refusal from the commandant Colonel [Christopher] Greene, the attack was undertaken at once. We took the outer defenses with little effort. This had hardly occurred when, because of the extensive losses and the indescribable cannonade and small arms fire from the fort and from the enemy ships lying on the water side, which fired on our right wing, and the almost impassable abatis before the main fort, plus the fascines being of little value at the eighteen-foot high parapet, necessitated a withdrawal without accomplishing our purpose. Our losses on dead and wounded totaled 397 men, and seven dead and fifteen wounded officers, among the last I am included, having a wound on my left heel and a bruise on my right thigh. Colonel von Donop, who was wounded in the right thigh also, Captain Wagner, and Lieutenant [Philipp Wilhelm] Heymel were captured. Of these losses, 112 men were from our regiment. As soon as we had again assembled, we marched in the already settling dusk, about eight miles, where we halted at midnight in order to bandage the seriously sounded. Many of these remained lying on the road because we had no wagons to transport them, and so they fell into enemy hands.

23 October - At two o'clock this morning we resumed our march again past Haddonfield, and about two o'clock in the afternoon arrived at the water. Here we met a corps of English Light Infantry which was to serve us as scouts. Since however, the commander of these troops had learned the bad news, that we had failed, from Lieutenant Pertot [Leopold Friedrich Bertaud ?] of the Wutginau Regiment, who had been sent ahead to carry the report to the commanding general, therefore they stopped us. The wounded however, were immediately transferred across to Philadelphia and quartered there. At three o'clock the 64-gun ship *Augusta*, which was engaged with the battery on Mud Island, blew up. In the house where the wounded were bandaged at twelve o'clock on this night, many had been left lying. Lieutenant Pertot, with some jaegers, risked returning to them, pressed some wagons, and fortunately brought them back to us.

Rueffer Journal

24 October - Yesterday evening all the regiments from New Jersey returned here and the Battalions Linsing, Lengercke, and Minnigerode and our regiment moved into the barracks. Colonel von Bock, [Heinrich von Borck], (of the Knyphausen Regiment) has been temporarily named commander of our regiment because our commander, Lieutenant Colonel von Schieck was killed. Today Lieutenant von Heister was sent to Fort Red Bank with a flag of truce in order to ask about Colonel von Donop, also to ask for his parole, which was refused out of hand, but granted the request that [Chaplain Georg Friedrich] Heller request the same of General Washington. Today we received a commendation because of the unfortunate failure of the attack that witnessed the good courage. The army stands here, close before Philadelphia, and has stretched a chain [of redoubts] from the Delaware to the Schuylkill. The English headquarters is in the city, the Hessians live in Hamilton's beautiful house.

Philadelphia is the capital city of Pennsylvania and has about 4,000 houses. The streets are laid out in parallel lines and it is three miles long and one mile wide. The city hall or Congress House is very large and beautiful and stands in the middle point of the city, according to the plan, as additions are to be built onto it. Not far from where it stands there is another beautiful stone building called the jail, where the sick and prisoners are guarded. The local barracks are large so that 1,800 persons can live therein. The churches are: two English, three meeting houses for the Quakers, two for the Presbyterians, one German Reform, one Swedish, one Catholic Church, as well as a meeting house for the Anti-baptists, and one for the Herrnhutter. Pennsylvania lies between 40^0 and 43^0 north latitude and 76^0 west longitude from London.

25 October - The wounded Lieutenant Schotten had his right arm amputated today.

26 October - Because Lieutenant von Heister brought the news back from Red Bank that Colonel von Donop was in danger of dying, also that the rebels had no surgeons for bandaging the wounded, Regimental Surgeons [Wilhelm] Pausch and Gechter were sent to Red Bank. It is said that Red Bank will be attacked again soon, using more heavy cannons. The army was notified today that General Vaughan had definitely captured the city of Esopus and set it on fire. He had also destroyed all the enemy artillery and burned all the enemy's magazines and ships.

27 October - The order arrived today that in a few days the army will be set in motion. Also the baggage ships were told to send the most necessary items to us.

28 October - We learned that after General Clinton's victories on the North River, he sent General Vaughan with 2,000 troops toward Albany in order to establish communications with General Burgoyne.

30 October - Captain Wagner, Lieutenant Heymel, and Regimental Surgeon Pausch arrived from Red Bank and brought the news that Colonel Donop died yesterday and was buried with military honors. Two hundred men marched out for his burial, of whom half fired three times. Also, three cannons were fired. The first two had to swear not to take up arms again until such time as they were exchanged. They gave high praise for the care and treatment provided by the enemy, not alone to Colonel von Donop, but to all the prisoners and wounded.

31 October - Our regiment moved out of the barracks and into camp in the line.

1 November - One no longer doubts that after several engagements with a superior force of the enemy, General Burgoyne has had to surrender due to a shortage of provisions. The prisoners, after giving their word that they would not again take up arms, were granted permission to go aboard ship and await orders from General Howe for their departure. Today an English sergeant was hanged for assaulting an officer.

2 November - Work progresses continuously to complete the line before the city, with ten redoubts, each for 200 men and two cannons.

3 November - Two floating batteries have been constructed to attack the forts on Mud Island and Red Bank.

4 November - Although we assume General Washington plans to attack our lines, we have remained quiet except for the outposts, which are frequently harassed.

5 November - Today a part of our regiment arrived from the ships which came from our fleet, which is still at Chester, to Providence Island on flatboats, having sneaked past the enemy's ships, with much danger. We work with the greatest exertions, especially at night, on the cannon and bomb batteries on Providence Island, which is not far from, and opposite, Mud Island, which in the meantime is being fired on from both sides.

7 November - It is reported with much certainty that the army of General Washington fired victory volleys three times: 1) Because of our unsuccessful attack on Fort Red Bank 2) That because of a mistake, the 64-gun ship *Augusta* blew up 3) That in New England a victory was gained over General Burgoyne.

8 November - From Lieutenant [George Preston] Vallancy of the 62nd Regiment, who brought a description, the unfortunate affair of General Burgoyne has been confirmed:

"Extract of a report from Lieutenant General Burgoyne to the Commanding General-in-Chief, Sir William Howe, dispatched 20 October 1777."

In accordance with my orders to strive with the greatest effort to proceed to Albany, I crossed the Hudson River to Saratoga on 13 September. Every means was sought. The army under my command fought twice against a far greater force. The first meeting was on 17 September, and after a four-hour battle, we held the field. The second, on 7 October, did not have such a fortunate outcome and ended with the enemy storming two of our detachments.

The one was defended by Colonel Breymann, who was killed on the spot and the post was lost. The other was defended by Lord Balacaras, leading the British Light Infantry, which the enemy, with great loss, overcame. Because the enemy occupied all the fords and passages on the east side of the Hudson River and our army could not move farther forward, we retired to the haven of Saratoga. Everyone awaited the [enemy] army and the opportunity for battle, and offered to engage the enemy on 13 October as they had only three days' rations remaining. At the same time, the last hope of timely relief disappeared. My strength as a result of the battles had sunk to 3,500 fighting men, of which 1,900 were British, surrounded by 16,000 enemy and on the general concurrence of the generals, field officers, and captains commanding corps, I was moved to open negotiations with Major General [Horatio] Gates. The army decided as one man to die rather than to do anything which ran against national or personal honor.

Convention Articles between Lieutenant General Burgoyne and Major General Gates:

1. The troops commanded by Lieutenant General Burgoyne are to march out of their camp with the honors of war, and the artillery from their positions, to the bank of the river where the old fort stood, and there the weapons and artillery are to be left. The weapons are to be stacked at the command of their own officers.

2. The army commanded by Lieutenant General Burgoyne shall be granted free passage to Great Britain with the stipulation that during the present war, they will not again serve in North America, and the port of Boston is designated for the transport ships to embark the troops as soon as this is ordered by General Howe.

3. Should an exchange be agreed upon, through which the army commanded by General Burgoyne, or a part

thereof, can be exchanged, the previous article will be invalidated in so far as such an exchange pertains.

4. The army commanded by Lieutenant General Burgoyne shall march over the easiest, closest, and most comfortable route to Massachusetts Bay and be quartered in, nearby, or as comfortable to Boston, so that the march of the troops will not be prolonged when transport ships come to load them.

5. The troops on their march and while in quarters will be provided in the same manner and with the same rations, by order of Major General Gates, as his own army, and when possible, the officers will be provided with fodder for their horses and cattle in the same manner.

6. All officers shall retain their wagons, pack horses, and livestock, and no baggage shall be taken nor searched, because General Burgoyne has pledged his honor that no public property has been hidden therein. Major General Gates will take the necessary measures to insure compliance with these articles. However, should there be a shortage of wagons to transport the officers' baggage during the march, they will be provided where possible by the inhabitants at the usual price.

7. During the march, and as long as the army is quartered in Massachusetts Bay, the officers, in so far as circumstances permit, will not be separated from their men, in order to be able to read lists of their names and other activities for maintaining order.

8. All corps of General Burgoyne's army, including sailors, boatmen, artisans, drovers, independent companies, and camp followers of the army, shall be included in the above articles to the fullest extent, and in all situations will be treated as British subjects.

9. All Canadians and persons who belong to the Canadian establishment, including sailors, boat people, artisans, drovers, independent companies, and any others

who follow the army and belong to no special service, shall be allowed to return by the shortest route to the first British post on Lake George, and shall be provided with provisions in the same manner as other troops, and shall make the same pledge not again to serve in this war in North America.

10. Three officers, of whom none shall have rank higher than captain, to be designated by Lieutenant General Burgoyne, shall be given guaranteed passes for carrying messages to Sir William Howe, Sir Guy Carleton, and to Great Britain by way of New York, and Major General Gates pledges the public trust that these letters shall not be opened and that these officers, as soon as they receive their letters, may set out by the shortest route, and travel by the quickest means.

11. As long as the troops remain in Massachusetts Bay, the officers shall be granted parole and permitted to keep their side arms.

12. Should the army commanded by Lieutenant General Burgoyne find it necessary to send to Canada for their clothing and other baggage, this will be permitted, using the same comfortable means, and the pertinent articles shall be signed and exchanged tomorrow at nine o'clock by both sides, and the troops commanded by Lieutenant General Burgoyne will march out of their lines at three o'clock in the afternoon.

In camp at Saratoga, 16 October 1777

Signed
Horatio Gates
Major General"

9 November - General Washington's army is reportedly thirteen miles from here and supposedly he has been at Fort Red Bank to thank the defenders for their proven resistance on 22 October.

11 November - We learned from an adjutant, who arrived with the fleet, that General [Robert] Pigot at Rhode Island had sent him to the commanding general with information that the rebels had made an attack on that island, but were beaten back with heavy losses.

12 November - As all the bomb and cannon batteries on Providence Island, as well as the floating batteries, are now complete, ten privates from each company of the Light Infantry, as well as the Grenadier Company and the English Guards, commanded by Colonel Osborn, marched to Providence Island in order to attack the batteries on Mud Island, with the help of the warships, by the most favorable wind. The 27th and 28th Regiments also marched there at the same time in order to assist Colonel Osborn, should the need arise.

13 November - Direct bomb hits on the Mud Island fort had started several fires, which were extinguished each time however. Since yesterday evening and throughout the entire day, the fort has been exceedingly heavily bombarded, but the enemy has not answered in a like manner.

14 November - Yesterday toward three o'clock there appeared in the vicinity of the city a rebel frigate and we assumed that it would begin a bombardment. However this morning it had returned to its fleet. The bombardment from Providence Island, against Mud Island, continued today, uninterrupted.

15 November - Today six warships, including the battery ship *Vigilant* and the so-called *Jorker* sloop, approached Mud Island and with the help of the batteries from Providence Island, cannonaded and bombarded it so strongly that the noise was comparable to a thunder storm. The fort returned few shots, therefore the ships, which lay in the neighborhood of Red Bank, fired all the more and despite the indescribable cannonade, still an enemy row galley risked traveling back and forth to Mud Island. In case the ships can not compel the fort to surrender today, the above mentioned troops already on Providence Island are to storm the fort tomorrow at four o'clock.

16 November - This morning, about two o'clock, the rebels evacuated Mud Island after having set the barracks on fire. The damage which the fort received from the ships and the bombardment from Providence Island, according to people who have seen it, is indescribable. There is no place a foot in length where one can walk, which has not been hit by a cannonball. The eighteen-foot thick parapet is so shot up that entrance ways have been cut through it. The house of the commandant has so many holes that more than a thousand can be counted and the floors are as blown up as when a herd of swine had been there. Above all, it was evacuated by the rebels in such a deplorable condition that it is as difficult to describe by word of mouth as it is in writing. The garrison, which consisted of 350 men, was evacuated about one o'clock at night to Red Bank. It had been commanded by [Colonel Henry Leonard Philip], Baron d'Arendt, who had previously been in Prussian service. They left sixteen heavy iron cannons behind, nine of which had been spiked, however. No single object was in one piece. The fort was built by the English during the previous war, but had been made nearly unconquerable by the rebels in this one. About the island they had stretched two strong chains, twisted about one another in the water so as to make it nearly impossible for boats to land. In addition, this chain was connected to the first row of *chevaux de frise*. Now the fort is occupied by an English regiment and will be repaired by our side. The rebels have thrown all their dead in the water, and of these, they had twenty on the fourteenth, and 41 on the fifteenth, and on these two days, 110 seriously wounded. The admiral of their fleet is a slovenly debtor, but has been an experienced English naval officer, and is named [John] Hazelwood. Noteworthy is the fact that one year ago today, Fort Knyphausen fell into our hands.

17 November - As now the clearing of the *chevaux de frise* is being carried on with the greatest effort, we hope to see our fleet here in the harbor very soon, because everything is so expensive, which as a consequence, creates a bad situation. For a bottle of wine, as well as for a pound of sugar, or a pound of coffee, one must pay one [the unit of cost is not clear], likewise one pound of meat or bread, which is very scarce, must be paid for at ten for the first and eighteen [groschen ?] for the last. It is said that a corps which General Clinton detached from New York had crossed into Jersey between Red Bank and Fort Billings[port] in order to capture the first one. This detachment reportedly was composed of two Ansbach and three English battalions, as well as the new Jaeger Company recently arrived from Hesse.

18 November - This past night, at eleven o'clock, the Lengercke Grenadier Battalion, as well as a detachment of Jaegers and some English regiments, marched and were to join the troops mentioned yesterday, in New Jersey. General Cornwallis commands the entire force which numbers about 6,000 men.

19 November - We hear that a row of the *chevaux de frise* has been removed and it is expected that the chain which stretches to the Delaware from Mud Island will be cut.

20 November - The rebels had not expected the attack on Red Bank, but fled on this night.

21 November - This morning at four o'clock we were disturbed by some cannon shots on the Delaware and we noticed that the rebels had set their entire fleet on fire. Some row galleys sought to travel past the frigate *Delaware*. Upon this being noticed, a heavy fire was laid down from both sides, causing the galleys to move away from there. It was a beautiful view to see so many ships drifting and swimming about on fire under a dark sky, and hearing the sound as still loaded cannons exploded. Under a flag of truce, our regimental surgeon returned again this afternoon from the rebels and confirmed that the rebels had evacuated Red Bank. He gave high praise to the rebels for their care of our prisoners, of whom only twenty of 63 still survive. Also, we learned that the force at Red Bank had been strengthened daily, that it finally reached a strength of 1,500 men, who were commanded by General Slocum, and which this day marched to Haddonfield after leaving Red Bank.

22 November - This morning about nine o'clock almost the entire line was alerted. A troop, about 200 strong, was so daring as to attack our right wing, which is about fifty yards from the city, and at once engage our forces. A battalion of Englanders immediately moved out and pursued them for several miles.

23 November - We learned from a spy that General Washington had been strengthened by 6,000 New Englanders. Captain Wagner, who was wounded at Red Bank, died of his wounds today.

24 November - There are already about twenty ships in the harbor of this city, still the cost of living will not go down

25 November - Concerning the corps in New Jersey, nothing is yet certain, but it has reportedly been engaged with the enemy.

26 November - The number of ships continues to increase daily and there are nearly 200 present, also the cost of living begins to lower somewhat.

27 November - All convalescents from the hospital at New York, as well as those on ships of both fleets, and a small transport of recruits were landed today.

Lieutenant [Dietrich] von Gottschall died today.

28 November - This afternoon the corps which had been in New Jersey under General Earl Cornwallis returned and we learned that he had demolished Fort Red Bank. Also, that the rebels yesterday morning, at daybreak stormed our new jaeger position, killed twelve and wounded 21. However, as soon as the grenadiers arrived, the enemy fled. Lieutenant [George Hermann] Heppe and Lieutenant von Hagen were severely wounded, and Lieutenant Heppe soon died therefrom. According to a Hessian officer, Lieutenant H., who was there,

Fort Red Bank had better defenses than we had been informed of prior to our attack. The trenches which were still visible and the parapets made such a strong defense as to be incomparable, both as to depth and width. The two Ansbach battalions have arrived here and have moved into the barracks.

29 November - The Combined Battalion received orders to be ready to embark. Eighteen thousand new Englanders are reported on the march and expected daily by General Washington.

30 November - There are many rumors that our regiment is to enter winter quarters in New York. The order for the Combined Battalion to embark was countermanded.

1 December - The cost of living still refuses to go down. it is still necessary to pay two Hessian guldens for one pound of butter, coffee, or sugar, or for a bottle or two of wine.

2 December - Today a fleet of fifty ships arrived here with provisions from Ireland.

3 December - The Combined Battalion has now lost this name, which was changed to the Woellworth Brigade, which was divided into two parts. Half from Woellworth and Major von Stein, and the rest of the Knyphausen Regiment, and the other half under Woellworth's command.

4 December - This morning at seven o'clock the army is to advance in two columns and only the 2nd English Brigade, the Woellworth Brigade, the 2nd Battalion of the 71st Regiment, the two Ansbach Battalions, and the Mirbach Regiment are to occupy the line.

4 December [sic] - At two o'clock this morning the army's order to march was countermanded because three English soldiers had deserted. Our Jaegers made a patrol six miles ahead and discovered that the enemy no longer occupied his previous outposts and made contact with them initially at two o'clock this afternoon, when a brief engagement occurred.

5 December - The army marched this past night at ten o'clock. The troops listed above, which were designated to occupy the line, remained here under the command of General Leslie. All heavy baggage has remained here. It is reported that during this expedition, Germantown and New Frankfurt are to be burned in order to drive the rebel army away from our winter quarters.

6 December - At two o'clock this morning we learned that the army had been engaged with the enemy and as the firing did not last very long, it is to be imagined that it was with their outposts.

7 December - Today a rebel general by the name of Ensign, [possibly James Irvine], a hat-maker by profession, born in Philadelphia, as well as some officers and a number of privates, was brought in as a prisoner. It is reported that the rebels made an attack on the pickets of our army. Still confirmation is required as to whether heavy and small arms fire was heard at about one o'clock.

8 December - There were many reports that a large corps of the enemy was between here and Germantown and therefore, the entire line moved out, from this morning until this afternoon. They had advanced as far as Chestnut Hill and Poeyssound but encountered the enemy in a situation so well fortified by nature and design that the commanding general decided that an attack would not succeed.

9 December - Since the army has again moved back into the line, the Ansbach Battalions again occupy the barracks. The entire Jaeger Corps received a commendation for its conduct during the last expedition and especially on the seventh. They suffered nine killed and nine wounded and the English Light Infantry lost about 100 altogether.

10 December - It is reported with considerable certainty that General Washington has left his fortified camp on Chestnut Hill. This morning at two o'clock General Cornwallis with a corps of 3,000 men and about 500 wagons, marched over the Schuylkill to the region of Darby to forage and drive in livestock. The local garrison is to consist of seventeen battalions this winter.

11 December - Today at noon our regiment received the order to embark tomorrow at seven o'clock, and to this end all baggage has been sent aboard ship. At seven o'clock this evening the order was countermanded.

12 December - This morning at two o'clock another large number of wagons followed after the corps commanded by General Cornwallis.

13 December - During the past night, the above mentioned corps returned with a large amount of livestock and forage. According to the order of General Howe, the horses of our regiment which were in good condition, were embarked. The two Ansbach Regiments entered winter quarters in the city today.

14 December - Today the baggage of His Excellence, General von Knyphausen, arrived from New York. It is reported that a merchant ship on the Delaware was inattentive to its course, and ran onto the *chevaux de frise* and sank. According to today's orders our regiment is to be debarked [embarked ?] tomorrow.

15 December - At one o'clock this afternoon our regiment, as well as the 2nd Battalion of the 71st Regiment, commenced embarking at Bruce's Wharf. Everyone was put on flatboats and sailed to Chester. The sick and wounded were put on a small, two-masted sloop with the name *Fanny*. The cabin was so small and miserable that our group, which consisted of seven people, could hardly turn around. At one-thirty we sailed with the ebb tide from Philadelphia. In the evening, at sunset, we passed the first row of *chevaux de frise* and Mud Island, but as it soon became too dark to see, we anchored at dusk.

16 December - We will never forget the night on this miserable sloop because the cabin of the sloop was so small and we could not go on deck. At nine o'clock this morning we raised anchor and at nine-thirty passed the frightful Red Bank.

At ten o'clock the last *chevaux de frise* and Billlingsport, which had been captured from the enemy by the Scottish detachment sent there from Wilmington on 1 October, without much resistance, were passed. At eleven-thirty we arrived at Chester and there learned that the fleet had already sailed. Nevertheless, we met it, to our great joy, at anchor between Marcus Hook and Wilmington, at three o'clock in the afternoon. After our arrival we were at once brought aboard our ship *Badger* and there met Captain Endemann, Ensign von Drach, and Ensign [Henrich] Abel of the Wissenbach Regiment. The assignments, since our group now numbered ten people, were as follows: *Wittby*: Colonel von Borck, Lieutenant von Toll, Ensigns Wiessenmueller, von Bulzingsloewen, and Abel of the Wissenbach Regiment, Regimental Quartermaster Schmidt, and Chaplain Virnau. *Charming Polly*: Major von Wilmowsky, Captains Reichhold and Rothe, Lieutenants Schraidt and von Boyneburg, and Ensign von Drach. *Badger*: Captain Endemann, Lieutenant Schotten, Ensign Berner, Regimental Surgeon Gechter, Auditor Heinemann, and me.

17 December - The 2nd Battalion of the 71st Regiment was transferred across to New Jersey today to get forage.

18 December - This evening the above mentioned battalion returned aboard ship with considerable forage and livestock.

19 December - At daybreak a signal was made to raise anchor, which happened, and we sailed immediately. We had gone only a few miles when we again had to anchor in the vicinity of Wilmington, due to a contrary and very strong wind. It was very cold but also very bright weather. At four o'clock we again raised the anchor and sailed with the ebb tide until seven o'clock in the evening.

20 December - Still beautiful weather, but cold. At daybreak we raised the anchor. At seven o'clock we passed New Castle. This city lies close to the Delaware, about forty miles up the bay, and 100 miles from both capes. It is the capital city of the three bordering counties on this river and contains

Ruaffer Journal

about 100 houses. These counties, New Castle, Sussex, and Kent, for a time belonged to Holland, but were given up by the Peace of Breda. Now they belong to Pennsylvania. Toward noon we met our escort frigate *Apollo*. On the Pennsylvania side we could see beautiful country homes. Toward evening we anchored again.

21 December - West-southwest wind, very favorable and at the same time a pleasant day. As soon as it became light we raised anchor. Toward two o'clock we could see the lighthouse and at four o'clock we had passed it and no longer sailed in Delaware Bay, but on the ocean. The wind grew stronger and better and if it continues to hold, we hope to anchor tomorrow evening at Sandy Hook, as it is only 129 miles from here.

22 December - West-southwest wind and stormy. We spent a very restless night, because the weather was so stormy. Although the wind is very strong, it is also favorable enough so that we can sail six or seven miles in an hour. Toward noon the wind became lighter and the sky brighter. Toward four o'clock, to our great joy, we could see the lighthouse at Sandy Hook and we anchored there at seven o'clock.

23 December - East-northeast wind and tolerable weather. Toward nine o'clock we raised the anchor, but because the wind was too contrary to enter the harbor, we had to allow our hopes of being in New York this evening to vanish and at six o'clock this evening we anchored near Long Island.

24 December - Still the contrary wind of yesterday. Nevertheless, we tried to get to New York. It continues very cold, but at the same time, the weather is very bright. All efforts to enter the harbor were in vain and again we had to anchor.

25 December - At six o'clock this morning we raised the anchor anew, but because of contrary winds, again had to drop it. At one o'clock the wind became more favorable and toward evening we arrived at New York. Lieutenant Schotten, Ensign Berner, Ship Surgeon [should be Regimental Surgeon] Gechter,

Auditor Heinemann, and I at once debarked and took lodgings at Grimm's Tavern.

26 December - The regiment still spent this day aboard ship. The 2nd Battalion of the 71st Regiment was sent to Staten Island.

27 December - This morning at one o'clock, the regiment debarked and entered winter quarters in the country on the North River, outside the city.

End of the 1st and 2nd Campaigns in America

New York, 28 December 1777

List

Officers belonging to the Hessian Corps who were lost during the period from the marching out of Hesse until the end of the second campaign, and specifically in 1776: [In addition to a sequence number, the regiment, and the individual's name, the German manuscript list has an overall heading of "how and by what means death occurred". This heading is broken down further to categories of "Killed", "wounded", "died of wounds" and "died of illness". Each category is again divided into columns headed "when" and "where". I have written out the list using only sequence number, regiment, name, and the additional information pertaining to the entry, as follows:

1) Jaeger Corps, Lieutenant [Friedrich Wilhelm] von Grothausen, died in New Jersey of wounds [possibly in January 1777].

2) Jaeger Corps, Lieutenant [Ernst Friedrich Wilhelm] von Donop, died of illness in New Jersey [in February 1777].

3) Minnigerode Grenadier Battalion, Captain [Georg Karl Ludwig] Hoepfner, died of illness in New York on 15 October 1776.

4) Lengercke Grenadier Battalion, Captain [Wilhelm] von Bentheim, died of illness on Long Island on 13 November 1776.

5) Lengercke Grenadier Battalion, Captain [Friedrich Karl] von Weitershausen, wounded 1 December 1776 in New Jersey, died of his wounds 2 December 1776 at Brunswick in New Jersey.

6) Leib Regiment, Captain [Count Simon Ludwig Wilhelm] von der Lippe, wounded in a duel aboard ship on 4 June 1776, died 5 June 1776 aboard ship.

7) Landgraf Regiment, Captain [Friedrich Moritz] Medern, wounded storming Fort Knyphausen [then Fort Washington] on 16 November 1776, and died of his wounds 19 November 1776 at Harlem on York Island.

8) Landgraf Regiment, Lieutenant [Georg Wilhelm] von Loewenfeld, wounded storming Fort Knyphausen on 16

November 1776, and died of his wounds on 17 November 1776 at Harlem on York Island. [Chaplain Waldeck of the Waldeck Regiment indicated in his diary that Loewenfeld died on the battlefield.]

9) Hereditary Prince Regiment, Captain [Matthias Arnold] Rueffer, died of illness at New York on 31 October 1776. [Brother of the author ?]

10) Prince Charles Regiment, Ensign [Adolf] von Herda, died of illness in a hospital on Long Island on 12 October 1776

11) Donop Regiment, Ensign [Franz Karl] von Staedel, died aboard ship at sea on 24 June 1776.

12) Lossberg Regiment, Colonel [Henrich Anton] von Heringen, died of illness on Long Island on 26 September 1776.

13) Lossberg Regiment, Captain [Johann Kaspar] Riess, killed at Trenton on 26 December 1776.

14) Lossberg Regiment, Captain [Friedrich Wilhelm] von Benning, killed at Trenton on 26 December 1776.

15) Lossberg Regiment, Lieutenant [Georg Christoph] Kimm, killed at Trenton on 26 December 1776.

16) Knyphausen Regiment, Major [Karl Friedrich] Dechow, wounded at Trenton on 26 December 1776, died of his wounds at Trenton on 28 December 1776.

17) Knyphausen Regiment, Captain [Wilhelm Henrich] von Barckhausen, wounded storming Fort Knyphausen on 16 November 1776, died of his wounds at Harlem on 19 November 1776.

18) Mirbach Regiment, Captain [Theodor Benjamin] Riess, died of illness on Staten Island on 24 August 1776.

19) Rall Regiment, Colonel [Johann Gottlieb] Rall, wounded at Trenton on 26 November [should be December] 1776 and died of his wounds on 27 November [should be December] 1776.

20) Rall Regiment, Captain [Johann Friedrich] Walter, killed at Fort Knyphausen on 16 November 1776.

21) Stein Regiment, Captain [Johann Friedrich] Rosencranz, died of illness at Mile Square [New York] on 5 November 1776.

22) Stein Regiment, Lieutenant [Johannes] Schwein, killed at Kingsbridge [New York] on 9 November 1776.

23) Wissenbach Regiment, Lieutenant Colonel [Johann Ernst] Lange, died at sea with the 2nd Division in May 1776.

24) Huyn Regiment, Lieutenant [Henrich Friedrich] Justi, killed at Fort Knyphausen on 16 November 1776.

During 1777

1) Artillery, Lieutenant [Christoph Ludwig] Diede, died of illness in a hospital on Long Island on 20 November 1777.

2) Jaeger Corps, Colonel [Karl Emil Ulrich] von Donop, wounded storming Fort Red Bank on 22 October 1777, and died of his wounds at Red Bank on 29 October 1777.

3) Jaeger Corps, Captain [Johann Friedrich Jakob] Trautvetter, wounded in action at Brandywine on 11 September 1777, and died of his wounds on the ship [name illegible, possibly *Lord Howe*] on 16 November 1777.

4) Jaeger Corps, Lieutenant [Georg Hermann] Heppe, wounded in New Jersey on 21 November 1777, and died of his wounds in New Jersey on 25 November 1777.

5) Linsing Grenadier Battalion, Captain [Johannes] von Groening, wounded at Red Bank on 22 October 1777, died of his wounds at Philadelphia on 23 October 1777.

6) Linsing Grenadier Battalion, Lieutenant [Konrad] DuPuy, killed at Red Bank on 22 October 1777.

7) Linsing Grenadier Battalion, Lieutenant [Dietrich] von Gottshall, wounded at Red Bank on 22 October 1777, died of his wounds at Philadelphia on 26 November 1777.

8) Minnigerode Grenadier Battalion, Captain [Johann Emanuel] Wagner, wounded at Red Bank on 22 October 1777, died of his wounds at Philadelphia on 22 November 1777.

9) Minnigerode Grenadier Battalion, Lieutenant [Georg Wilhelm] Hille, killed at Red Bank on 22 October 1777.

Rueffer Journal

10)   Minnigerode Grenadier Battalion, Lieutenant [Karl] von Offenbach, killed at Red Bank on 22 October 1777.

11)   Landgraf Regiment, Lieutenant [Henrich Julius] von Lindau, wounded at Fort Knyphausen on 16 November 1776, died of his wounds on 26 January 1777.

12)   Hereditary Prince Regiment, Captain [Ludwig] Winckelmann, died of illness in New York on 4 April 1777.

13)   Truembach Regiment, Ensign [Christian Friedrich August] Cleve, wounded in a duel at Kingsbridge on 16 February 1777, died of his wounds.

14)   Truembach Regiment, Lieutenant [Theodor Friedrich] von Buttlar [and] Treusch, died of illness at New York on 3 September 1777.

15)   Mirbach Regiment, Lieutenant Colonel [Ernst Rudolf] von Schieck, killed in the attack on Fort Red Bank on 22 October 1777.

16)   Mirbach Regiment, Lieutenant [Wilhelm Erdmann] von Bogatzky, killed in the attack on Fort Red Bank on 22 October 1777.

17)   Mirbach Regiment, Lieutenant [Johann Konrad] Riemann, killed in the attack on Fort Red Bank on 22 October 1777.

18)   Mirbach Regiment, Lieutenant [Karl Friedrich] von Wurmb, killed in the attack on Fort Red Bank on 22 October 1777.

19)   Rall Regiment, Lieutenant Colonel [Balthasar] Brethauer, died of illness as a prisoner of war at Winchester [Virginia] on 24 September 1777.

20)   Rall Regiment, Captain [Johann Friedrich] Sternickel, died of illness as a prisoner of war at Winchester on 10 September 1777.

21)   Rall Regiment, Captain [Johann Henrich] Bruebach, died of illness as a prisoner of war at Dumfries [Virginia] on 18 March 1777.

22) Wissenbach Regiment, Captain [Georg] Stoebel, committed suicide at New York by cutting his throat, on 28 May 1777.

23) Wissenbach Regiment, Lieutenant [Johann Jakob] Scheffer, died of illness at New York on 24 February 1777.

24) Wissenbach Regiment, Ensign [Ludwig] Ernst, died of illness at Kingsbridge on 26 February 1777.

25) Huyn Regiment, Captain [Johann Henrich Zacharias] Wagner, committed suicide at New York by cutting his throat on 12 May 1777.

26) Buenau Regiment, Major [Philipp Christian] Mell, died of illness at Rhode Island on 3 November 1777.

27) Buenau Regiment, Lieutenant [Johannes] Wiegand, died of illness at Rhode Island on 6 March 1777.

TRAUTVETTER, Johann Friedrich 91
Johann Friedrich Jakob 121
TREUSCH, Theodor Friedrich
Vonbuttlar and 122
TRYON, Gov 69 William 65
TUFFIN, Charles Armand 88
VALLANCY, George Preston 105
VAUGHAN, Gen 104 John 73
VAUPEL, Johann Nikolaus 66
VIRNAU, Chaplain 12 18 20 99 116
Rudolph Reinhard 71
VONBARCKHAUSEN, Wilhelm
Henrich 120
VONBAUMBACH, Lt 91
VONBENNING, Friedrich Wilhelm
61 120
VONBENTHEIM, Wilhelm 119
VONBIESENRODT, Hans Friedrich 3
35 Hans Moritz 34 Lt 26 29 Lt Col
26 28 29 Maj 71 73
VONBIESENROTH, Lt Col 28
VONBOCK, Col 103
VONBODE, Carl 29
VONBODESTSKY, Ensign 26
VONBOGATZKY, Capt 12 18 19 99
Wilhelm Erdmann 3 34 122
VONBORCK, Col 20 22 87 116
Heinrich 20 103
VONBOYNEBURG, Lt 12 18 20 71
99 116 Ludwig Wilhelm August 3
35
VONBULZINGSLOEWEN, Ensign 18
116 Karl Wilhelm 4 35 Lt 26 29
VONBUTTLAR, and Treusch Theodor
Friedrich 122 Theodor Friedrich
122
VONDECHOW, Karl Friedrich 66
VONDERLIPPE, Simon Ludwig
Wilhelm 50 119
VONDIEMAR, Ernst Friedrick 23
VONDONOP, Col 19 52 85 101 102
103 104 Ernst Friedrich Wilhelm
119 Karl Emil Ulrich 19 52 121 Lt
52
VONDRACH, Ensign 5 12 18 20 71
99 116 Erhard 3 Ernst 35 Lt 26 29
Wilhelm 4 36
VONEHRENSTEIN, Carl 26

VONESCHWEGE, Friedrich 56
VONFORSTNER, Karl 91
VONGEYSO, Ludwig Ferdinand 66
VONGOTTSCHALL, Dietrich 35 112
VONGOTTSHALL, Dietrich 121
VONGROENING, Johannes 121
VONGROTHAUSEN, Friedrich
Wilhelm 119
VONHACKENBERG, Karl Wilhelm
59
VONHAGEN, Lt 112
VONHEISTER, Gen 50 53 55 58 60
Leopold 9 Leopold Philipp 36 Lt
103 Lt Gen 3 65 73
VONHERDA, Adolph 120
VONHERINGEN, Henrich Anton 120
VONKEUDEL, Henrich Walrab 28
VONKNYPHAUSEN, Gen 16 59 60
89 90 91 100 115 Lt Gen 16 20 62
65 73 76 77 85 86 88 Wilhelm 11
Wilhelm Freiherr 59
VONLENGERCKE, Georg Emanuel
28 68
VONLINDAU, Henrich Julius 122
VONLINSING, Otto Christian
Wilhelm 28
VONLOEWENFELD, Georg Wilhelm
119
VONLOOS, Col 17 35 63 68 74 93 94
95 Johann August 3 34
VONLOSSBERG, Friedrich Wilhelm
27
VONMIRBACH, Gen 7 9 27 37 47
Maj Gen 14 65 Werner 3 34
VONMUENCHHAUSEN, Friedrich
13 Friedrich Ernst 73
VONOFFENBACH, Karl 122
VONOLDERHAUSEN, Herr 35
VONPRUESCHENCK, Adam Ernst
Carl 24
VONRAU, Karl 61
VONROMRODT, Christian 22 Col 25
26 29
VONSCHIECK, Col 19 68 99 Ernst
Rudolph 3 34 122 Lt 5 Lt Col 12
13 18 20 59 67 71 72 103
VONSTAEDEL, Franz Karl 120
VONSTEIN, Maj 96 113

VONTOLL, Capt 26 29 Karl Henrich 3
35 Lt 12 18 20 71 99 116
VONWANGENHEIM, Friedrich Adam
Julius 98 Lt 99
VONWEITERSHAUSEN, Friedrich
Karl 119
VONWILMOWSKY, Alexander 67
Capt 73 Col 29 Lt Col 26 Maj 18
20 99 116
VONWISSENROTH, Abel 20
VONWURMB, Carl Friedrich 35 Gen
27 28 Karl Friedrich 3 122 Lt 5 12
18 19 44 45 47 71 99 Ludwig
Johann August 88
WAGNER, Capt 102 104 112 Johann
Emanuel 19 121 Johann Friedrich
Zacharias 68 Johann Henrich
Zacharias 123 Johnn Emanual 101
WALDECK, Chaplain 120 Gottlieb 61
WALDENBERG, Peter Michael 49

WALTER, Johann Friedrich 120
WASHINGTON, 22 Gen 24 25 91 92
94 95 97 103 105 108 112 113 114
George 24
WAYNE, Anthony 93
WELSH, 91
WEMMES, Gen 93
WERNER, Lt 60
WIEDERHOLD, Andreas 4 36 Lt 5
WIEGAND, Johannes 123
WIESSENMUELLER, Ensign 5 12 18
20 71 99 116 Johann Georg 3 35 Lt
25 26
WILMOWSKY, Maj 85
WILSON, Lt 86
WINCKELMANN, Ludwig 122
WOELLWORTH, 113
WURMB, Lt 46 48
ZIMMERMANN, Henrich Christoph
66

Other books by the author:

Eighteenth Century America (A Hessian Report On the People, the Land, the War) As Noted in the Diary of Chaplain Philipp Waldeck (1776-1780)
Enemy Views: The American Revolutionary War as Recorded by the Hessian Participants
Hessian Chaplains: Their Diaries and Duties
Hesse-Hanau Order Books, A Diary and Roster: A Collection of Items Concerning the Hesse-Hanau Contingent of "Hessians" Fighting Against the American Colonists in the Revolutionary War
Most Illustrious Hereditary Prince: Letters to Their Prince from Members of Hesse-Hanau Military Contingent in the Service of England During the American Revolution
Order Book of the Hesse-Cassel von Mirbach Regiment
A Hessian Officer's Diary of the American Revolution Translated From An Anonymous Ansbach-Bayreuth Diary and The Prechtel Diary
Journal of the Hesse-Cassel Jaeger Corps
Journal of a Hessian Grenadier Battalion
Hessian Letters and Journals and A Memoir
The Trenton Commanders: Johann Gottlieb Rall and George Washington, as noted in Hessian Diaries
Defeat, Disaster, and Dedication
Revolutionary War Letters Written by Hessian Officers: Generals Wilhelm von Knyphausen, Carl Wilhelm Von Hachenberg, Friedrich Wilhelm von Lossberg, Johann Friedrich Cochenhausen, Friedrich Von Riedesel and Major Carl Leopold von Baurmeister
English Army and Navy Lists, Compiled During the American Revolutionary War by Ansbach-Bayreuth Lieutenant Johann Ernst Prechtel
Journal of the Prince Charles Regiment
The Diary of Lieutenant von Bardeleben and Other von Donop Regiment
Georg Pausch's Journal and Reports of the Campaign in America, as Translated from the German Manuscript in the Lidgerwood Collection in the Morristown Historical Park Archives, Morristown, N.J.

CD: The Hessian Collection, Volume 1: Revolutionary War Era
CD: Diaries of Two Ansbach Jaegers
CD: Waldeck Soldiers of The American Revolutionary War
CD: Canada During the America Revolutionary War
CD: A Hessian Report on the People, the Land, the War of Eighteenth Century America, As Noted in the Diary of Chaplain Philipp Waldeck 1776-1780
CD: They Also Served. Women with the Hessian Auxiliaries
CD: A Hessian Diary of the American Revolution
CD: A Hessian Officer's Diary of The American Revolution
CD: Ansbach-Bayreuth Diaries from the Revolutionary War

www.ingramcontent.com/pod-product-compliance
Lightning Source LLC
Chambersburg PA
CBHW071810090426
42737CB00012B/2022